COLLINS LIVING HISTORY

The Great War 1914-1918

Peter Fisher
Series editor: Christopher Culpin

Collins Educational
An imprint of HarperCollinsPublishers

Contents

UNIT 1	Europe on war alert	6
UNIT 2	Trench warfare	12
UNIT 3	On the home front	24
UNIT 4	On the battle front	36
UNIT 5	The aftermath	50
	Glossary	62
	Index	63

attainment target 1

Questions aimed at this attainment target find out how much you know and understand about the past. Some questions are about how things were different in history: not only people's food and clothes, but their beliefs too. Others are about how things change through history. They may change quickly or slowly. They may change a great deal or only a little. Other questions ask you to explain why things were different in the past, and why changes took place.

attainment target 2

This attainment target is about understanding what people say about the past. Historians, as well as many other people, try to describe what the past was like. Sometimes they say different things. This attainment target is about understanding these differences and why they occur.

attainment target 3

This attainment target is about historical sources and how we use them to find out about the past. Some questions are about the historical evidence we can get from sources. Others ask you about how valuable this evidence might be.

Introduction

'When I was about 14, I became very interested in the Great War. I remember watching a long television series about the war. There were many questions which I wanted to ask my elderly stepfather, Arthur Foxlee. He had fought in the trenches, but to my surprise, he was unwilling to talk about his experiences. I wondered what he had been through. My stepfather's reluctance to talk was not unusual. A German writer was interviewed in a recent television documentary about the Great War. He said that his father, Ludvig Harig, "never talked about his war, when he was questioned, he just stood there breathing hard with his eyes bulging and never saying a word". Arthur Foxlee and Ludvig Harig and millions of other British and German soldiers, like those in the photograph below, were made enemies in 1914 by the Great War.'

Peter Fisher

This book looks at the Great War as a major turning point in history. It focuses on Britain's role in the wider European struggle. As you read through this book and look at the sources, you may begin to understand why soldiers from the Great War, like Arthur Foxlee and Ludvig Harig, stayed silent, unable to talk about the war.

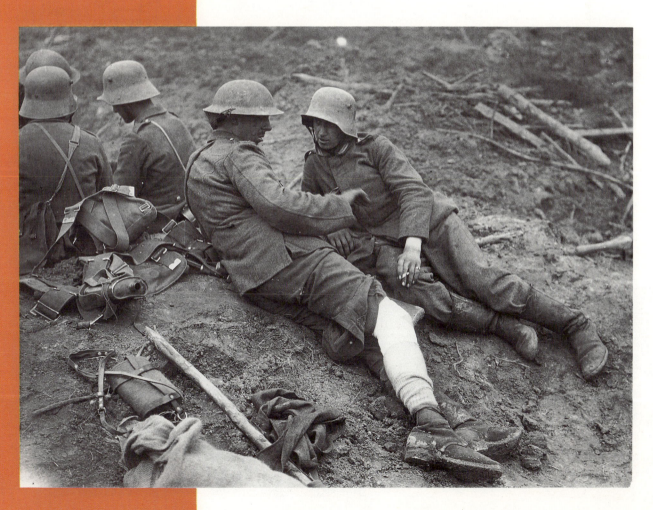

'25 January 1918. The school will be closed from Monday the 28th till Friday February 1st to enable teachers to assist in preparing 'ration' cards, a preliminary to the local introduction of a 'rationing' scheme as from March 4th.'

'18 October 1918. Owing to the need for saving fuel, the school hours from Monday the 21st until further notice will be as follows: morning session 8.45 am to 11.45 am, afternoon session 1.00 pm to 3.30 pm. The time table will be advanced accordingly.'

'28 October 1918. Owing to the depletion of staff in the junior department – influenza epidemic – Miss Lyall and Mr Threlfall are temporarily doing duty there from today.'

'8 November 1918. Upwards of 90 children absent each time the school was open – influenza epidemic.'

SOURCE 1
Extracts taken from the log book for Priory Street Boys' School, Gateshead.

'School was completely done away with. There was only one school master who taught in private in a flat. I wound up leaving school when I was 10½.'

SOURCE 2
A French civilian remembers the German occupation of the Somme.

SOURCE 4
Children from a school in Reims wearing their gas masks.

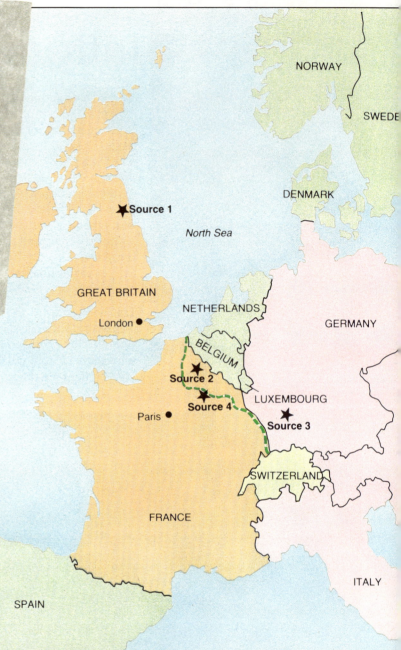

'Kantorek had been our school master, 'the terror of Klosterberg'. During drill-time Kantorek gave us long lectures until the whole of our class went, under his shepherding, to the District Commandant and volunteered. I can see him now, as he used to glare at us through his spectacles and say in a moving voice: "Won't you join up, Comrades?".'

SOURCE 3
An extract from E. M. Remarque's novel *All Quiet on the Western Front*, written in 1929. The book is set in southern Germany.

This map shows the two 'armed camps' in Europe in the summer of 1914. It also shows the position of the Great War's major fronts which were developed by December 1914.

ACTIVITIES

Throughout this book, you will be encouraged to talk about the sources. On these two pages, we will look at a range of sources which relate to the experiences of children during the Great War. If you look at the questions, you will see that the same sources can be used to help you with different lines of enquiry.

An enquiry into historical sources

1 Divide your class into four groups so that each group can look at one of the sources on these two pages. You could then ask the following questions about your group's source.
- Is it a primary or a secondary source about children and the Great War?
- Is it based on an eye-witness or a second-hand account?
- Is it a record or a recollection?
- How reliable is your source?

2 Then, as a whole class discussion, you could compare Sources 1 to 4, and think about how reliable they are as pieces of historical evidence.

An enquiry into civilian life during the Great War

1 How could Source 1 be used to begin an enquiry into the effects of shortages, rationing and the flu epidemic in 1918?

2 Using Source 4 as a starting point, try to find out what precautions civilians had to take during the Great War.

3 Using all the sources on these two pages, you could start thinking about the lives of civilians from Britain, France and Germany and compare how much they were changed by the Great War.

An enquiry into children's lives during the war

1 Study Source 3. Try to find out what children in Britain, France and Germany were taught about their own country and its empire before 1914. How might the attitudes they were taught at school have encouraged young people to enlist in 1914 when war broke out?

2 Compare Sources 1 to 4. How much impact do you think the Great War had on schoolchildren living in France, Germany and Britain?

UNIT 1

AIMS

Why did Arthur Foxlee, a British citizen, and Ludvig Harig, from Germany, find themselves enemies in 1914? How did they feel about their own country? What prompted them to join up? In this unit we shall see why countries in Europe went to war in 1914; we shall find out which countries were rivals and which were ALLIES. We shall discover the long-term causes of conflict in Europe and also look at the key events in 1914 and why they led to war.

Europe on war alert

In March 1992, the British Royal Navy launched its first Trident nuclear submarine, HMS *Vanguard*, see Source 1. It represented the very latest in military technology. In 1906, Britain's HMS *Dreadnought* was regarded as the most advanced battleship of its day. The size, speed and fire power of HMS *Dreadnought* made all other battleships out of date.

In 1908, Germany responded by launching its own dreadnought battleship – SMS *Westfalen*, see Source 2. As each of the European powers built up their fleets, the naval arms race gathered speed. The way the German sailor is treated in Source 3 illustrates the rivalry between the great European powers. Source 4 shows the resources of each of them. There is no single or simple cause for the outbreak of the Great War. Instead, we need to look at a combination of causes.

SOURCE 1
Britain's first Trident submarine, HMS *Vanguard*, 4 March 1992.

SOURCE 2
The first German dreadnought, SMS *Westfalen*, launched in 1908.

SOURCE 3
A cartoon from *Punch* magazine. Mr Punch, the photographer, is speaking to the German sailor: 'Just a little further back, please, Sir. Your shadow still interferes with the group'.

---

1. Which of the following descriptions do you think is most accurate for Source 1 and Source 2? Give reasons for your choice in each case.
   - An aggressive, threatening weapon, ready for war.
   - A defensive weapon for maintaining peace.
   - A demonstration of economic power and military technology.
   - A symbol of national pride.

2. Look at Source 3. What pre-war issue is this cartoon about? What can you learn from it about friendships, jealousies and fears?

Friends and foes

There were many rivalries in the pre-war years. France had lost valuable areas of land to Germany in 1871 and swore revenge. Austria-Hungary and Russia competed for power over the Balkans (this region is shown in Source 6 on page 8). Both Germany and Italy had emerged as new nations in the 1870s after long struggles for UNIFICATION. At the start of the 20th century, they were anxious to assert themselves. They wanted to develop overseas empires and trading networks to match those of the more established European powers, like France and Britain. Other peoples in central and eastern European countries wanted nationhood. The old sprawling Ottoman and Austro-Hungarian empires embraced many nationalities. Nationalism would lead to these empires breaking to pieces, so their leaders tried to crush it.

Alliances

Countries tried to protect themselves by promising military assistance to each other if they were attacked. A system of agreements, creating two 'armed camps' in Europe, had been set up well before 1914. The most important were the Triple Alliance of 1882 which linked Germany, Austria-Hungary and Italy and the 'Triple Entente' of 1907 which linked France, Britain and Russia.

This structure of alliances, together with the arms race, meant that a spark, a single event, could escalate into war. Friends would 'fall in' against foes in an automatic way. Let's now look at events in 1914 that would be the turning points which would lead these two 'armed camps' into the Great War.

SOURCE 4
The resources of the main European powers before the Great War.

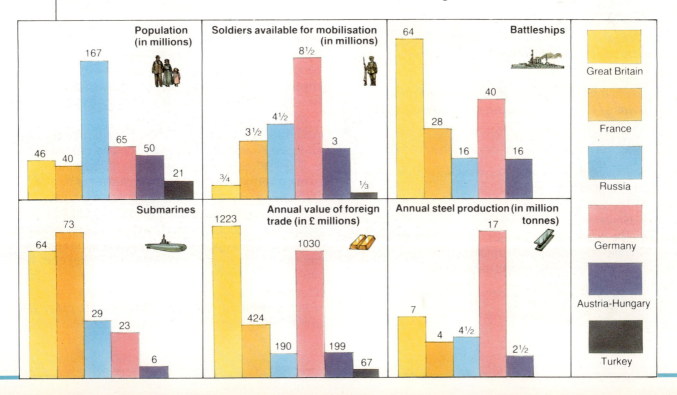

EUROPE ON WAR ALERT

Ferdinand and the fatal shot

Looking at the events of the summer of 1914 from today, war seems to be the inevitable result. But we have the advantage of hindsight: we know the outcome. The politicians and generals who made the decisions did not. Who decided that war should come? What was the turning point?

As Source 5 shows, nationalist rivalries between ethnic groups in the Balkans – the Serbs, Croats and Bosnians – erupted into civil war in 1991. Nationalist feelings were equally strong in 1914, when the people of Bosnia, mainly Serbs, were ruled as part of the vast Austro-Hungarian empire. You can see the extent of this empire in Source 6.

SOURCE 6
The Balkans in 1914.

SOURCE 5
Yugoslav army soldiers resting in a trench on a hillside in Bosnia near the border with Serbia in 1992.

Shots in Sarajevo

On 28 June 1914, the Bosnian capital, Sarajevo, played host to a royal visit from Archduke Franz Ferdinand and his wife Countess Sophie on their wedding anniversary. The Archduke was heir to the throne of the Austro-Hungarian empire. Crowds of people thronged the streets of Sarajevo to cheer the royal couple, but among them were Bosnians who fiercely resented imperial rule from Austria-Hungary. A group of students had plotted to assassinate the Archduke, see Source 7. Gavrilo Princip fired the fatal shots and was immediately arrested by the police.

The leaders of the Austro-Hungarian empire blamed Serbia. Austria-Hungary consulted its ally, Germany, and issued Serbia with an ULTIMATUM: Austria-Hungary threatened to go to war unless Serbia admitted involvement in the Sarajevo episode.

Serbia called upon Russia for protection. This was not the first crisis in the Balkans, but earlier ones had often been solved by diplomacy (international talks). This time, to add pressure, orders for troops to MOBILISE went out. Long-prepared plans to move vast armies into position by rail were put into action.

---

attainment target 1

Look at pages 6 to 9 before you answer these questions.

1. List as many reasons as you can why the great powers of Europe were close to war with each other for some time before 1914.

2. What new reasons for war developed in 1914?

3. Which of the following do you think was the most important reason for war?
   - The Schlieffen Plan.
   - Nationalism.
   - The alliances.

   Choose one reason and explain your choice. Compare your choices with each other.

4. Who do you think was to blame for the outbreak of the Great War?

EUROPE ON WAR ALERT

The Schlieffen Plan

The German war plan which was put into action by Kaiser Wilhelm II had been drawn up by Alfred von Schlieffen in 1905, see Source 8. Although the plan was updated and amended, it made a number of assumptions, some of which turned out to be wrong. These were as follows:

- Germany had always planned to attack France first, whatever the circumstances. They expected to defeat France before the Russians were ready to mobilise their army.

- The Schlieffen Plan involved German troops marching through NEUTRAL Belgium. In 1839, Britain had agreed to protect Belgium's right to be neutral, but Germany calculated that this old agreement would not be enough to pull Britain into war.

War breaks out

The Schlieffen Plan left no time for diplomacy to avoid war. On 1 August 1914, Germany declared war on Russia and, on 3 August, on France. Germany's decision to cross Belgian borders had serious consequences. The Kaiser dismissed the document signed by the British in 1839 as no more than a 'scrap of paper'. But, as German troops marched on Belgium on 4 August, Britain declared war. The alliance system was called into play and Europe was at war.

> 'One young conspirator failed to draw his revolver; another felt sorry for the Archduke's wife and went home; a third threw his bomb, and missed. The Archduke reached the Town Hall. He was now angry; his wife's treat had been spoilt. He decided to drive straight out of town. But his chauffeur was not told. He took the wrong turning, then stopped the car and reversed. Gavrilo Princip, one of the schoolboys, saw before him, to his amazement, the stationary car. He stepped on to the running-board; killed the Archduke with only one shot ... and hit the Archduke's wife with a second. She too, died almost immediately. Such was the assassination at Sarajevo.'

SOURCE 7
A modern historian recounts the assassination of Archduke Franz Ferdinand.

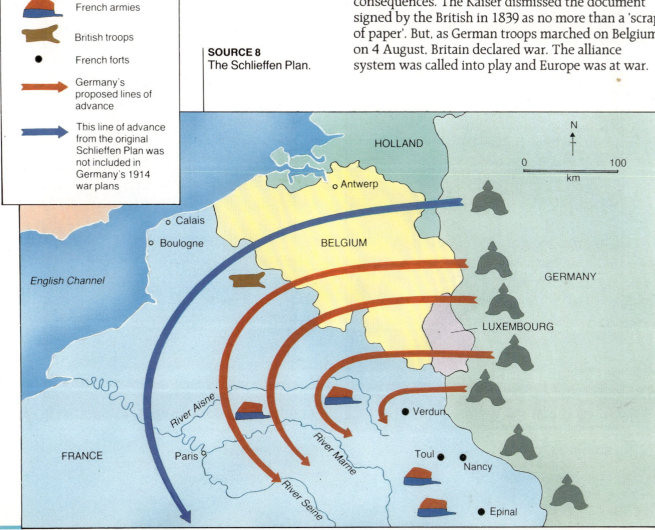

SOURCE 8
The Schlieffen Plan.

Legend:
- German armies
- French armies
- British troops
- French forts
- Germany's proposed lines of advance
- This line of advance from the original Schlieffen Plan was not included in Germany's 1914 war plans

EUROPE ON WAR ALERT

Fervour and force

The outbreak of the Great War was greeted with enthusiasm across much of Europe. People responded quickly to the 'call to arms', eager to show their sense of national pride and PATRIOTISM see Source 9. In Britain, many people expected the war to be over by Christmas, so men were eager to volunteer immediately. Amid the optimism, the British Secretary of State for War, Lord Kitchener, warned that the conflict could be long and bloody.

Recruitment

A massive recruitment campaign was launched, using posters like those shown in Sources 10 and 11. Some of the posters appealed to feelings of patriotism, others to fears of guilt or embarrassment. Recruiting poetry was published in the national press. The poems often compared war to a 'sport' or a 'game' as shown in Source 12, but these feelings were to sound hollow within a few weeks. The eventual response to the appeal for 100,000 men was overwhelming. Two and a half million men volunteered in 1914 to 1915. Some of the motives for joining up are expressed in Source 13.

SOURCE 9
This monument from Newcastle-upon-Tyne, called 'The Response', was unveiled in 1923.

SOURCE 10
Images of home were used to encourage people to join the army (enlist).

SOURCE 11
The Great War's most memorable image of mobilisation.

EUROPE ON WAR ALERT

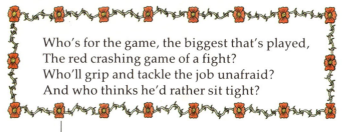

Who's for the game, the biggest that's played,
The red crashing game of a fight?
Who'll grip and tackle the job unafraid?
And who thinks he'd rather sit tight?

SOURCE 12
The opening verse from Jessie Pope's poem, 'Who's for the game?'.

Mobilising troops

Troops were mobilised all over Europe and DEPLOYED to the areas of assembly already mapped out by each country's war plans. Soldiers and supplies were moved as far as possible by rail, but the last few kilometres of the journey to the battle areas had to be made on foot, see Source 14. Soldiers would sing rousing songs like 'It's a long way to Tipperary' to help them keep up with the official marching pace of five kilometres per hour.

Once they arrived at the front, the troops drew strength from the justice of their cause. At the same time, there was a gradual realisation of the dangers and horrors they were about to face.

> We said that we would serve. We offered ourselves. Call it patriotism. To every man and nation comes the moment to decide for truth or falsehood.
>
> 'Cos I got fed up with the foreman on the farm.
>
> King and Parliament had decided upon it. That was all we needed.
>
> I was quite empty headed ... and bored to tears with shop life ... the chaps round about started to go, so I said 'I'm going'.
>
> Well it was gonna be a change ... most volunteers went to get away from their environment.

SOURCE 13
Recollections of enlistment.

1 Did the pre-war alliances and war plans make the Great War inevitable?

2 List the reasons why men enlisted in 1914. Copy the table below and list your reasons under the two headings.

Pull factors	Push factors

3 What emotions were Sources 10 and 11 designed to appeal to?

SOURCE 14
The march to war.

UNIT 2

Trench warfare

AIMS

In this unit we will look at why and how the Great War was dominated by trench warfare. We shall look at the attempts to break the deadlock of the trenches and bring some movement to the battlefields. We will then consider the impact of trench warfare upon the lives of soldiers in the firing line. We will also look at how different types of sources and battlefield evidence can be used to help us understand the nature of trench warfare.

H. G. Wells wrote *The War of the Worlds* in 1898, see Source 1. Although it was a work of science fiction, some of the predictions which H. G. Wells made did have similarities with the Great War. He described a future world where mechanical weapons would destroy thousands of human lives and vast expanses of land. These descriptions seemed fantastic to readers at the end of the 19th century. Yet in less than two decades these descriptions were to become the realities of war.

Before the outbreak of war in 1914, forecasts about the scale and nature of the fighting differed among military leaders and politicians. Looking back, a key question which historians ask is how far could (and should) the coming of trench warfare have been predicted in 1914? Some historians argue that military leaders expected the war to be no different from earlier ones. As Source 2 reveals, military training was based on this prediction. Other historians claim that military leaders should have been better prepared, especially after the experiences of the American Civil War in the 1860s, the Boer War of 1899 to 1902 and the Russo-Japanese War of 1904 to 1905.

These wars had already demonstrated the power of ARTILLERY and rapid-fire machine guns to inflict heavy casualties. They had also revealed the tactical importance of strong defences: attacks on such defences had resulted in heavy loss of life. Source 3, written by a Polish banker called Ivan Bloch in the 1890s, is a remarkably accurate prediction of how the Great War would unfold.

SOURCE 1
A compact disc cover from the musical adaptation of *The War of the Worlds*. Based on the novel by H.G. Wells, the soundtrack was first released in 1978.

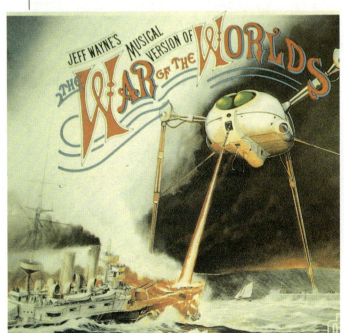

'It must be accepted that the rifle, effective as it is, cannot replace the effect produced by the speed of the horse, the charge and the terror of cold steel.'
Cavalry Training Manual, 1907.

'Close with the enemy, cost what it may. A determined and steady advance lowers the fighting spirit of the enemy.'
Infantry Regulations, from about 1910.

'The way out of what looks like an impossible situation is by attack. The moral effect is enormous.'
Army Textbook, from about 1910.

SOURCE 2
Extracts from training manuals which did little to prepare soldiers for the realities of the Great War.

> The distance is 6000 metres from the enemy. Shells tear up the soil and burst over the head of the enemy, raining down hundreds of fragments and bullets over his position.... Now they are but 2000 metres away.... The firing lines will advance one after another.... Yet, with all this movement between the two armies, there will be a belt 1000 paces wide separating them as by neutral territory swept by the fire of both sides.... Everybody will be entrenched in the next war. The spade will be as indispensible to the soldier as his rifle. The first thing a soldier will have to do ... will be to dig a hole in the ground and throw up a strong earthern rampart to shield him. ... The ammunition will be almost exhausted, but the fire will continue until the empty ammunition cases are replaced by full.... The moment will approach when half the combatants will be mown down. Dead and wounded will lie in parallel rows separated by that belt of 1000 paces ... which no living thing can pass.

SOURCE 3
Ivan Bloch's vision of future warfare, written in the 1890s.

SOURCE 4
French troops resisting the German advance in September 1914.

ACTIVITY

Look at Source 3. Draw a diagram of a battlefield showing the features which Ivan Bloch predicted. You should include a scale to show distances and a key for any symbols which you use. Compare your results with the diagram of a battlefield on page 38 and the Copymaster trench map in the Teacher's Notes.

Plans and action

Once the war began, French and German plans were put straight into action, look back at Source 8 on page 9. Germany's Schlieffen Plan was designed to capture Paris by a speedy advance through neutral Belgium. The Germans knew that France would have to be defeated within six weeks. Troops would then be ready to defend Germany against Russian armies attacking on the Eastern Front.

At first, all went well for Germany. It was later that problems arose: the Belgian army fought strongly and delayed the progress of the German attack. Then British troops arrived in support of Belgium's neutrality.

The French war plan, called Plan XVII, was designed to strike at Germany's armies from a fortified border, but it failed. French and British troops resisted the German advance towards Paris, as shown in Source 4. In September, Germany was forced into retreat – the Schlieffen Plan had failed. To avoid being driven further back, the Germans dug themselves into quickly prepared trenches defended with machine guns and artillery, see Source 5. The Allies responded by doing the same. Both sides 'raced to the sea' to try to get round the ends of each other's lines. This ended in October with the last battle of movement on the Western Front, at Ypres in Belgium. After that, both sides dug in and any hopes of the war being 'over by Christmas' faded away. The realities of trench warfare had arrived.

SOURCE 5
German troops preparing their first trenches.

SOURCE 7
German troops attacking on the Eastern Front.

Fronts

Source 6 describes two unique features of the Western Front – its narrowness and its length. Both sides remained deadlocked on the Western Front for over three years, at a cost of over 8,200,000 lives.

The Eastern Front

The Eastern Front lay between the borders of Germany, Austria and Russia, see pages 4 to 5. The speed with which the vast Russian army was mobilised surprised Germany's leaders. They had to divert their troops from the Western Front to force Russian armies out of German territory. German and Austrian troops were able to prevent the poorly equipped Russian forces from advancing. The Eastern Front had its own problems: harsh winter weather and the vast distances involved. In spite of these problems, Germany was more willing to launch major offensives along the Eastern Front than in the west. The Eastern Front also became deadlocked by the end of 1914, although it was not as immobile as the Western Front. There was a less developed system of trenches and there were fewer troops 'holding the line'. This meant that when either side mounted an attack, limited movements of the front line were possible, see Source 7.

> 'Space voyagers would have been able to spot the Western Front, though they might also have been surprised by its narrowness. Soldiers withdrawing a mere matter of ten miles from it would find themselves in a world where the war had never been.'

SOURCE 6
An extract from a modern commentator on the Great War.

SOURCE 8
The fate of the cavalry – a dead Indian soldier and his horse, March 1918.

TRENCH WARFARE

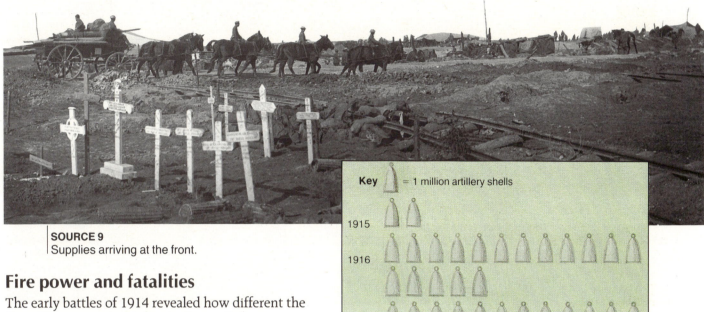

SOURCE 9
Supplies arriving at the front.

Fire power and fatalities

The early battles of 1914 revealed how different the Great War was going to be. As Source 8 shows, cavalry attacks proved useless against modern artillery and rapid-fire weapons. With the developing trench system, CAVALRY attacks could only be used after the INFANTRY had managed to break through enemy positions. This was easier to plan on paper than to carry out. Both sides became deadlocked. It was much easier for each side to hold on to its defensive positions than to attack and capture enemy positions.

SOURCE 10
British shell production during the Great War.

Supplies

Trench warfare required vast and constant supplies of weapons and AMMUNITION, see Source 9. Developing and producing weapons depended upon technological and scientific research. In addition, huge resources of land, labour, money and enterprise were needed to sustain the war effort. As the deadlock persisted, factories worked even harder to produce the MUNITIONS needed to continue the war, see Source 10. A well-organised transport network was also needed to make sure that supplies arrived at the front on a regular basis.

The key weapons

Machine guns and heavy artillery were the deadliest weapons of the Great War, see Source 11. It was difficult to capture enemy machine guns if they were protected by a dense network of barbed wire or enclosed within a fortified concrete 'pillbox'. The only way to escape their murderous fire was to 'dig in'. Heavy artillery was used for bombarding enemy trenches before an infantry attack, but often it churned up the ground and slowed down the advance of the infantry.

Against these weapons, self-defence became all-important, and each side created complex networks of trenches. Machine guns and heavy artillery were therefore largely responsible for the deadlock of trench warfare.

SOURCE 11
This detail from a painting by C.R.W. Nevinson shows a French machine-gun crew.

TRENCH WARFARE

SOURCE 12
'Gassed' painted by John Singer Sargent.

SOURCE 13
The old and the new: a horse and tank at Péronne, France in March 1918.

SOURCE 14
A mine explosion at Hawthorn Ridge, 1 July 1916.

Attempts to break the deadlock

Both sides set about inventing weapons which would break the deadlock on the battlefield. The two most important innovations were the gas attack and the tank, see Sources 12 and 13. Chlorine poison gas was first used at Ypres in Belgium, in April 1915. The German chemical industry was usually first to develop new types of gas but both sides used poison gas to support their infantry attacks. However, gas attacks failed to achieve a major breakthrough on the Western Front, because both sides took careful precautions against their deadly effects.

Tanks

Although Lord Kitchener at first dismissed the tank as 'a pretty, mechanical toy', other military leaders realised their potential. They could be used as armoured, mobile, gun platforms. They could crush barbed wire and withstand machine-gun fire. Expectations therefore ran high when tanks were first used on the Somme, in northern France, in September 1916. However, the new weapon had not been battle-tested. Not enough tanks were brought into action and they did not live up to expectations. As ground conditions on the battlefields worsened through the winter of 1916 to 1917, it was difficult to operate heavy tanks. However, when tanks were used on firm ground at Cambrai in 1917, 378 fighting tanks cut a six kilometre hole in the German positions. After this, British and French tanks were used in every major operation. This caused the German general Lüdendorff to call them 'our most dangerous enemies'.

TRENCH WARFARE

New dimensions

How could enemy lines be reached? Each side tried to attack enemy positions from below ground. They tunnelled under NO-MAN'S-LAND, placing mines and attempting to destroy enemy positions using high explosives, see Source 14.

Above ground, aeroplanes brought new hopes of breaking the deadlock. At first, they were used for RECONNAISSANCE to view the ground. They replaced the cavalry as 'the eyes of the army'. Planes quickly became important weapons of attack. Ground troops found it very difficult to defend and conceal themselves against air attacks.

The impact of war

The constant artillery bombardment devastated the landscape, as Source 15 shows. The impact of war on people was equally damaging. Some war artists portrayed the Great War soldier as an unbeatable fighting machine, see Source 16. In reality, of course, flesh and blood were no match for bullet and bomb. Troops felt helpless under the deadly artillery barrages, as described in Source 17. There was also a constant fear of gas attacks which had horrible effects. Not only did troops suffer from the enemy, there was also the tension, uncertainty and danger of mounting their own attacks – going 'over the top'.

attainment target 1

You will need to look at pages 14 to 17 before you answer these questions.

1. In groups of four, brainstorm the main points from these pages on a large sheet of paper. From your ideas, choose the key factors which you think led to deadlock and destruction in the trenches.

2. In pairs, draw a spider diagram to show the links between industrial society and the technological demands of the Great War.

3. Do you think any of the new weapons used in the Great War (poison gas, tanks, aircraft) acted as a turning point in bringing movement back to the battlefield?

SOURCE 15
'The Menin Road' painted by Paul Nash, 1919.

SOURCE 16
This sketch by the German artist Otto Dix is titled 'This is how I looked as a soldier'.

'We are now at Carskerke and the shrapnel (the splinters from shells) is screaming over our heads and the big guns are booming all at once. The German shells are falling quite close and it is just like hell itself – one's head is absolutely splitting with the din. Oh what a life. To think we could ever be here in the midst of things like this. The noise is too bad to continue – we are waiting here for wounded.'

SOURCE 17
An extract from Mairi Chisholm's diary entry for 24 October 1914. She was a nurse working close to the front line.

TRENCH WARFARE

Fire step and funk hole

Trench warfare created its own routines. In one month a soldier might spend four days in the front line, four days in the support line, eight days in reserve and 14 days 'resting'. These periods of 'rest' were often taken up with army tasks (FATIGUES) such as fetching and carrying wood, wire and water to keep the trenches in good order.

The front line routine

Troops holding front-line positions had to be continually alert to the possibility of enemy attack, see Source 18. However, the long periods of inactivity in the appalling trench conditions were also hard to endure as Source 19 explains. Each day started with 'stand to', half an hour before dawn, when all men waited with rifles at the ready. After dawn, one SENTRY per PLATOON remained on the FIRE STEP. The others would go to the DUGOUT to receive their daily rations. In Source 20, you can see soldiers resting in funk holes in the trench wall.

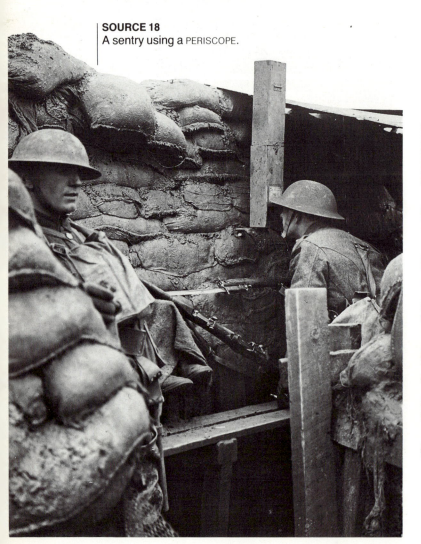

SOURCE 18
A sentry using a PERISCOPE.

The rota of duties

After breakfast, the sergeant in charge of each platoon would organise a rota of duties. For those on sentry duty, the tension of standing still for several hours at a time without losing concentration for a moment was exhausting. Of those who were not on sentry duty, some were sent to the support and reserve trenches to pick up more rations. The others were entitled to 'rest', see Source 21. However, there were still more jobs to be done: digging, filling sandbags, replacing DUCKBOARDS, strengthening the barbed wire defences and carrying ammunition. The day ended with another stand to at dusk. The ration parties returned under the cover of darkness with fresh supplies from the reserve trenches.

Activity at night

Trench activity increased at night. Small patrols were sent out into no-man's-land under the cover of darkness. They attempted to discover details about enemy resources and strength. Sometimes, full-scale trench raids were mounted to capture prisoners and gather information about enemy plans and positions. To guard against such night-time activities, both sides kept men on sentry duty at night and regularly lit up the night sky with star shells to reveal any trace of troop movements in no-man's-land.

---

1 Use the sources on these two pages to design a 24 hour clock diagram of the trench routine.

You stand in a trench of vile stinking mud
And the bitter cold wind freezes your blood
Then the guns open up and flames light the sky
And, as you watch, rats go scuttling by.

The men in the dugouts are quiet for a time
Trying to sleep midst the stench and the slime
The moon is just showing from over the hill
And the dead on the wire hang silent and still.

A sniper's bullet wings close to your head
As you wistfully think of a comfortable bed
But now a dirty blanket has to suffice
And more often than not it is crawling with lice.

SOURCE 19
This poem was written by Sidney Chaplin who served in the Gloucestershire Regiment.

TRENCH WARFARE

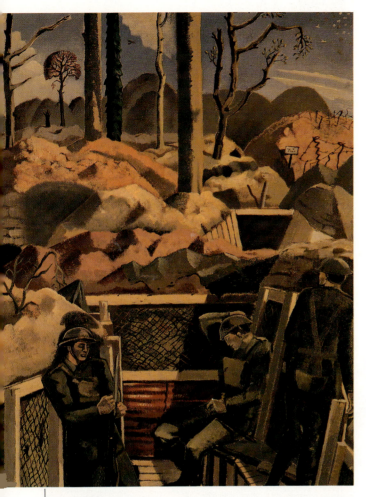

SOURCE 20
In this painting by Paul Nash you can see soldiers resting in their funk holes. In the foreground a sentry is standing on the fire step.

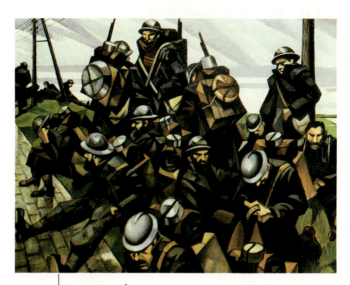

SOURCE 21
This painting by C.R.W. Nevinson shows French troops resting.

'Many men got trench feet and trench fever. With trench fever a fellow had a very high temperature, you could see he had. It wasn't dysentery but he had constant diarrhoea, it left him weak and listless. Trench feet was owing to the wet sogging through your boots. In many cases your toes nearly rotted off in your boots. We lost more that way than we did from wounds. Then again it was difficult getting them back through all this muck and sludge.'

SOURCE 22
Captain Burke of the Devonshire Regiment explains the common medical problems affecting troops in the trenches.

Trench conditions

Conditions in the trenches were often made worse by bad weather. Heavy SHELLING, coupled with rain or snow, made the trenches muddy and waterlogged. The trenches became infested with lice and rats and disease spread quickly among the troops, as you can read in Source 22.

The men serving on the front line felt a strong sense of togetherness in the face of all these problems. Yet in spite of the shared squalor and dangers of trench life, different living quarters and rations were issued according to rank. In turn, rank reflected pre-war social divisions based upon birth, education, occupation and wealth. Some have said that the war was a 'melting-pot', in which these class distinctions were broken down. The evidence of MEMOIRS, such as Source 23, shows that this was not really true: the social divisions remained.

It's queer, I thought, how little one really knows about the men. In the line one finds out which are the duds, and one builds up a sort of comradeship with the tough and willing ones. But back in billets (living quarters) the gap widens and one can't do much to cheer them up. I could never understand how they managed to keep as cheery as they did through such drudgery and discomfort, with nothing to look forward to but going over the top or being moved up to Flanders again.

SOURCE 23
An extract from *Memoirs of an Infantry Officer*, written by Siegfried Sassoon in 1930.

TRENCH WARFARE

Fellowship and faith

In Unit 1 we saw why people volunteered to join the army, but what made them stay in the trenches? A strong feeling of comradeship was certainly an important factor. Soldiers did not want to let their mates down, having shared the dangers of war together, as Source 24 reveals.

Live and let live

All troops had their orders to kill the enemy, but this did not mean that the two sides hated each other. Mutual suffering meant that both sides shared a kind of brotherhood. During the spontaneous Christmas truce of 1914, soldiers from either side of no-man's-land met to enjoy a brief period of FRATERNISATION, see Source 25.

1. How do you think the army commanders would react to the episode shown in Source 25?
2. How do you think a 'live and let live' system of trench warfare might work?
3. Make a list of the duties of an army chaplain serving in the trenches.

'Out here, dear, we're all pals. What one hasn't got the other has. We share each other's troubles, get each other out of danger. You wouldn't believe the humanity between men out here.... It's a lovely thing, is friendship out here.'

SOURCE 24
A letter written home by Private Mudd and dated 22 October 1917. Four days later he was killed.

SOURCE 25
British and German soldiers photographed during the Christmas truce of 1914. German soldiers crossed no-man's-land at dawn on Christmas Day singing carols and carrying gifts. Along some parts of the Western Front the truce lasted for nearly a week.

SOURCE 26
An army chaplain conducting a service from a bomber aircraft in 1918.

Chaplains

Army chaplains had to work in difficult circumstances, see Source 26. It was their duty to lift the morale of the troops during the long periods of routine and boredom. In the tension before an attack, the chaplains tried to reassure those about to go 'over the top'. In the aftermath of the fighting, they gave comfort to the wounded, the dying and those who had seen their companions killed.

Chaplains from Catholic, Anglican and Non-conformist churches and Jewish chaplains all served at the front. It is difficult to assess the role of these chaplains, and the chaplains themselves often questioned their value. However, there is no doubt that men responded best to those who worked close to the front and suffered with them.

TRENCH WARFARE

Fiascos

The scale of the war made massive demands on munitions. As armies grew in size, and the prospects of a short war faded, the need for more and more munitions created shortages of supply. In Britain, these shortages led to a row over who was responsible. You can read one of the arguments in Source 27. The generals blamed the government, and the government blamed munition workers. This was unfair because industry faced many difficulties adapting to wartime production.

> 'He (Kitchener) is firmly convinced that we waste ammunitions here. Wherever he put the new armies the same conditions prevail: a free expenditure of ammunition was the only way by which the infantry attack could be prepared. Trenches must be broken down, wire entanglements torn up, machine-gun resistance reduced by artillery fire and an unlimited amount of ammunition.'

SOURCE 27
An extract from the diary of Sir John French, the Commander-in-Chief of the British forces.

SOURCE 29
This painting by Norman Wilkinson shows the Allied landing at Suvla Bay.

Gallipoli

The Allies faced another major problem in 1915. Some military and political leaders believed that an offensive should be mounted against Turkey (one of Germany's allies) in the Aegean, see Source 28. This would open up possibilities to attack Germany from the east and break the deadlock. A vast force of 70,000 Allied troops was assembled, including many volunteers from Australia and New Zealand. However, troops landing on the Gallipoli peninsula became stuck on its narrow beaches and rocky cliffs. They suffered heavy losses from Turkish bombardments and counter-attacks, see Source 29. As summer approached, water shortages and swarms of flies caused sickness among the troops. The bitter winter conditions which followed reduced the Allies' ability to fight still further and a decision was taken to evacuate the troops.

The whole campaign was one of blunder and failure, but it made one thing clear. From early in 1916, political and military leaders who were keen to open up new fronts would have to argue their case that offensives like Gallipoli were more than just 'sideshows'. It was clear that the Great War would be won and lost on the Western Front.

Failure at Gallipoli, together with the supplies crisis on the Western Front, shook British confidence in the Liberal Government. The Prime Minister, Herbert Asquith, was forced to merge his government into an all-party COALITION government run by a war cabinet. David Lloyd George took on a key role as Minister for Munitions.

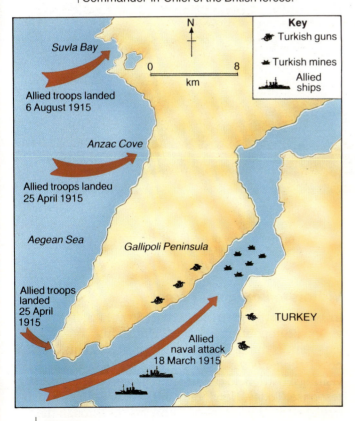

SOURCE 28
The Gallipoli campaign of 1915.

TRENCH WARFARE

Fields and forts

Today, many of the battlefields of the Great War have become areas of farmland, but each year there is still a 'harvest of iron', see Source 30. Sometimes the harvest is deadly. There have been a number of cases of farmers who have been killed by ploughing up live shells.

How can the study of field evidence help us to understand the nature of the Great War? The heavy fighting was confined to the narrow Western Front, see page 14. As a result, certain areas now provide a treasure trove for battlefield archaeologists. Each RELIC may reveal something about an individual soldier, about life under fire, or about a particular site and its part in the wider context of the war.

SOURCE 30
The 'harvest of iron': live shells awaiting removal by the French army.

SOURCE 31
Original trenches at Newfoundland Memorial Park.

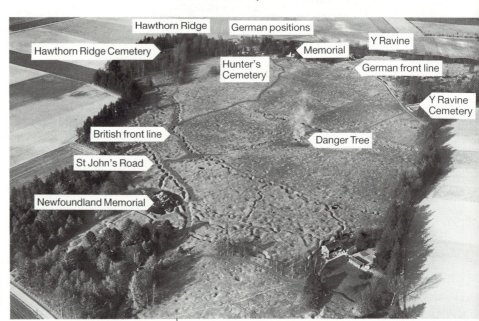

SOURCE 32
An aerial view of a preserved battlefield at Newfoundland Memorial Park.

Newfoundland Memorial Park

During the war there were thousands of kilometres of trenches along the Western Front. Today, only a few survive and even fewer are in their original condition. There is a good example of a small section of original battlefield at the Newfoundland Memorial Park near Beaumont Hamel on the Somme, see Sources 31 and 32. It was the site of a British and Canadian attack on German positions on 1 July 1916, see page 39. The trench lines are so well preserved because the site was bought by the Newfoundland government in memory of its 710 casualties. Field evidence from Beaumont Hamel, together with primary sources (such as trench maps, oral TESTIMONIES and written accounts) can help to explain the events of the battles which were fought there.

Visitors to Beaumont Hamel

In 1924, the American novelist, F. Scott Fitzgerald, visited Beaumont Hamel. He described his experiences through one of the characters in his novel *Tender is the Night*. As Source 33 shows, visiting a battlefield can release a powerful emotional response. Today, Newfoundland Park is well-managed for visitors. Neat pathways cut through the grass-covered shell holes and the zig-zagging trench lines, but as Source 34 reveals, it is still haunted by the grim events of 1916.

TRENCH WARFARE

> 'Dick turned the corner of the traverse and continued along the trench walking on the duckboard. He came to a periscope, looked through it a moment, then he got up on the step and peered over the parapet. In front of him beneath a dingy sky was Beaumont Hamel.... 'This land here cost twenty lives a foot that summer,' he said to Rosemary.... 'See that little stream – we could walk to it in two minutes. It took the British a month to walk it – a whole Empire walking very slowly, dying in front and pushing forward behind.''

SOURCE 33
An extract from *Tender is the Night*, written by F. Scott Fitzgerald in 1934.

'It was late July and, as I wandered across the shell torn slopes towards the German lines, the sound of thunder was heard in the distance, getting gradually nearer as might an artillery barrage. The light grew dim and black clouds gathered overhead. Lightning streaked across the sky – a veritable reincarnation of what a barrage must have been like.... After the hot day, the usual smell of rain-soaked grass began to permeate my nostrils ... but with a difference ... I realised that this was the smell of battle.'

SOURCE 34
An extract from *Before Endeavours Fade*, written by Rose Coombs in 1976.

SOURCE 35
A modern photograph of Fort de Moulainville, near Verdun.

Battlefield wastelands

There are some battlefields in France where the ground was so badly damaged that attempts failed to restore farming after the war. They have become wastelands.

During 11 months in 1916, the area around Verdun suffered massive bombardment from 40 million shells. Nine villages were destroyed, never to be rebuilt. It is still a wilderness. Battered remains of forts and remnants of a complex maze of tunnels survive in the forests, see Source 35.

Studies of the battlefield ARCHAEOLOGY at Verdun can give insights into the nature of the fighting there in 1916. They can also help our understanding of the arguments which took place in France after the Great War about the effectiveness of forts as a means of defence. Field evidence from Verdun can be used to compare the battles which were fought to take control of the fortified defences with trench warfare used elsewhere on the Western Front.

attainment target 3

1. The trenches in Source 31 are in their original positions, but not in their original state. What features are missing? Use the text and sources on pages 18 to 19 to help you.

2. Use Source 32 to mark the following features onto the trench map Copymaster in the Teacher's Notes:
   - British front line.
   - German front line.
   - No-man's-land.

3. The sites shown on these two pages are all original ones. Elsewhere on the Western Front, there are sections of trenches which are reconstructions or replicas of the originals. Do you think it is better to use original pieces of evidence, or copies, or both to understand the Great War? Give reasons for your answers.

4. What is the value of studying surviving sites from the Great War?
   - Is it in using them as sources?
   - Is it in using the sites as a stimulus to our emotions?

UNIT 3

On the home front

AIMS

In this unit we will look at how the war changed the lives of millions of CIVILIANS. The new technologies of warfare brought this war home more than any other. People were affected either directly, by living under the fear of death, or indirectly, by the changes which the Great War brought to everyday life.

Throughout the unit, we will look closely at the different views of the Great War held by civilians and soldiers. We will also see how women's lives and attitudes were changed by the Great War.

On 16 December, 1914, Bertie Young from Hartlepool arrived at school as normal. Like all his school friends, Bertie had been told that the war would be over by Christmas. He never found out. That morning he was fatally wounded by a splinter from a shell fired six kilometres away from a German battleship, SMS *Seydlitz*. He died the same day. Altogether, 121 civilians were killed during the attacks on Hartlepool.

Whitby and Scarborough were also bombarded by German ships of the High Seas Fleet. People in these towns were afraid of a German invasion on the east coast of Britain. They looked to the Royal Navy to defend them. Where was the Navy in December 1914? It was anchored 800 kilometres away at Scapa Flow. The German attacks were designed to lure the Royal Navy away from its main base at Scapa Flow but, as Source 1 shows, both fleets tried to avoid direct conflict. The closest they came to a decisive battle was at Jutland in June 1916, see Source 2. Without control of the North Sea, Germany never had any serious intentions of invading Britain, but public fears of invasion persisted in spite of this. Defences operated by mobile forces were put up along the east coast of Britain.

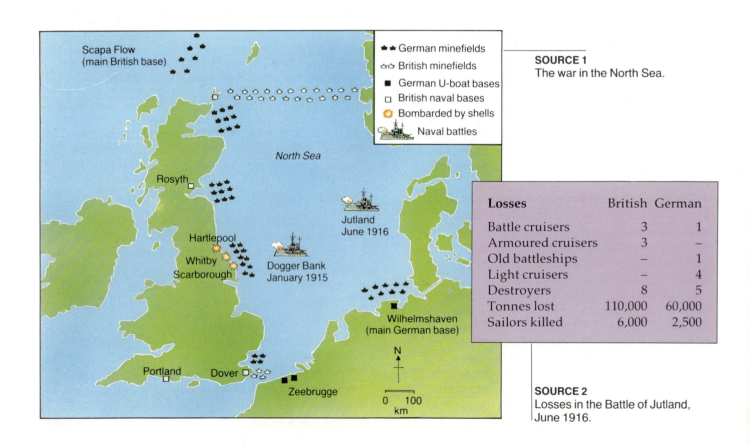

SOURCE 1
The war in the North Sea.

Losses	British	German
Battle cruisers	3	1
Armoured cruisers	3	–
Old battleships	–	1
Light cruisers	–	4
Destroyers	8	5
Tonnes lost	110,000	60,000
Sailors killed	6,000	2,500

SOURCE 2
Losses in the Battle of Jutland, June 1916.

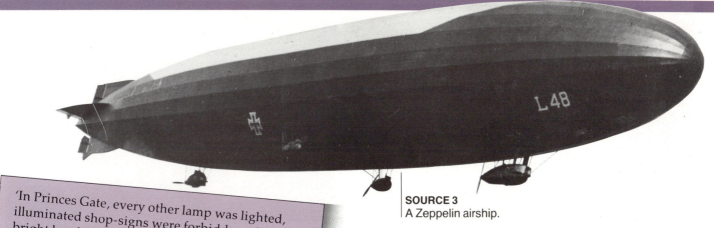

SOURCE 3
A Zeppelin airship.

'In Princes Gate, every other lamp was lighted, illuminated shop-signs were forbidden, also bright head-lights on motor cars. Blinds had to be pulled down as soon as the lights were lit, the penalties for breaking the rules were pretty severe. People began to make preparations for Zeppelin raids: one big wine dealer let several of his cellars. Most people had water or buckets of sand or fire extinguishers on every landing.'

SOURCE 4
A London resident, Winifred Tower, recalls the blackouts.

1 Do the figures in Source 2 confirm the view that the Battle of Jutland was a 'dead heat'?
2 Why did attack from the air come as a shock to the British people?
3 What were the reactions of the French, shown in Source 5, to the Zeppelin raids on Paris?

Zeppelins

Another threat to British civilians was the Zeppelin, see Source 3. As soon as the war began, public pressure in Germany mounted to send Zeppelins on night raids to destroy British military targets. It was also hoped that the Zeppelins would frighten civilians in Britain and weaken their will to work in support of the Allied war effort.

The first Zeppelin raids did indeed frighten the British population. Living on an island could no longer protect the British people from the dangers of the Great War. By April 1915, London was being attacked by Zeppelins. Strict blackout regulations and other precautions were enforced, see Source 4.

Public anger towards the Zeppelin menace grew because of the apparent lack of an effective defence. The first Zeppelin was not shot down until 3 September, 1916. Home Defence units of the Royal Flying Corps were then organised. Patrols were set up to intercept the Zeppelins as they flew towards London along regular flight-paths. The hydrogen filled Zeppelins burst into flames when they were hit and their crews burned to death.

In all, 57 Zeppelin raids on Britain killed 564 civilians and caused injury to 1,370 people. Zeppelin attacks were also mounted against France, see Source 5. In 1917 and 1918, Germany launched a new series of air-raids on Britain, using Gotha and Giant bomber aircraft. These caused greater loss of life and damage than the Zeppelins.

SOURCE 5
This painting by Robert Bonfils is titled 'The arrival of the Zeppelins' and shows the first Zeppelin raid on Paris.

ON THE HOME FRONT

Fact or fiction?

Today, television pictures of war can be sent around the world into our homes. During the Great War, information about the fighting was not easily available. It was difficult for civilians to build up a picture of what trench warfare was like. Civilians, even those close enough to hear the rumble of gunfire in France, received second-hand, sometimes distorted, reports of the war. Replica trenches were built for civilians to look at, see Source 6. Other images of the trenches came from soldiers' messages home, see Source 7. However, the soldiers themselves often found it hard to describe their experiences to relatives. There was a 'gap' in experience between soldiers and civilians which could not be bridged by media images and reports.

SOURCE 6
People from Berlin study replica trenches.

SOURCE 7
An embroidered postcard used to send news home from France.

'The issues of the English papers published in France are totally different from the issues published in England. The French papers are much better, being extremely good and truthful. The sum of it is that an English paper's report of a battle is full in the firing-line edition, is slightly censored when it gets to the base; and severely mutilated by the censor before it appears in England.'

SOURCE 8
An extract from Reverend Andrew Clark's diary for 12 August 1916.

Reports and propaganda

Civilians relied on the media for most of their information about the Great War. By the time the Great War broke out, improved education had led to a rise in the number of people who could read and write. Newspapers and magazines increased their circulation and influence. Press reports usually presented a positive image of the fighting. Once the deadlock developed, governments used the media to influence public opinion. They censored the press so that it became a channel for their PROPAGANDA, see Source 8.

At the same time, cartoons, stories and posters were used to fuel public hostility towards the enemy. Events which sparked off public anger, such as the first Zeppelin raids and the sinking of the *Lusitania* in 1915 were exploited to the full. These events were seized upon as proof of the German KULTUR, see Source 9. Propaganda was also designed to influence the public in neutral countries, especially the USA.

SOURCE 9
'The beastly Hun' – an American propaganda poster.

DORA

The war gave governments the opportunity to involve themselves in people's private beliefs and attitudes. In Britain, the Defence of the Realm Act (DORA) was passed in 1914. It gave the government wide powers over the individual citizen. It calmed civilian fears about contact with foreigners, and tried to stop the war rumours and spy stories which spread everywhere. Soldiers' letters to their families were censored, so that military information helpful to the enemy could be controlled. As Source 10 shows, this censorship was resented by some soldiers.

'I am not allowed to tell you where I am, because the General is afraid you might tell someone at school, and he might tell the German master, and the German master might telegraph to the Kaiser and tell him. And then, of course, the Kaiser would send an aeroplane to drop bombs on us.'

SOURCE 10
An extract from a letter written by Robert Scott Macfie in 1914.

Visual images

Visual images of the war came from army photographers who supplied the media at home, see Source 11. Unofficial photography, such as Source 25 on page 20, was banned at the front. Actual battle scenes were rarely recorded by photographers, because of the risks involved. The British public had to rely on artists' impressions like Source 25 on page 32. Both official and unofficial war artists served in the army. You can see examples of their work throughout this book.

Later in the war, cinema newsreels of events were produced. Again, there were obvious practical problems of filming battles, so some of the scenes were actually filmed during training exercises. This raises questions about the reliability of using such films as evidence. You can read more about this on pages 40 to 41.

SOURCE 11
This official photograph showing British gas casualties was taken by Tom Aitken.

1. Have modern communications made it easier for civilians to get information in wartime? (You could look at the media coverage of a recent conflict such as the Gulf War in 1991.)

2. Study Sources 6 to 8. What impression of the war does each one give? Compare them with Source 30 on page 45.

3. Work in pairs for this question. Why did governments use propaganda and censorship? Find a good example of propaganda in this book. What is its appeal and why is it effective?

4. Study Source 25 on page 20. Why were such photographs discouraged by the army?

5. Compare the images of war presented by Source 11 with Source 12 on page 16.
   - What are the similarities and differences?
   - Which image is more accurate?
   - Which has more impact?

ON THE HOME FRONT

Factory and field

The Great War was not an all-male affair. It changed the lives of both sexes. Women were expected to continue their traditional role of keeping the home together, in spite of the strain of being separated from their loved ones. In addition, millions of women worked in the factories and on the farms to help the war effort.

Women were active in many ways. When war was declared, recruitment propaganda exploited the patriotic 'duty' of women to encourage men to volunteer. Women organised the provision of 'comforts' for the troops. These included a total of 232 million cigarettes, 16 million books and four million pairs of socks. Women also helped with refugees and joined organisations like the Voluntary Aid Detachment. Some women served on the front while others campaigned vigorously in the 'fight for peace'.

By 1915, the mood of women had changed. Many demanded the 'right to serve' like the men. With shell shortages and a constant need for more men at the front, the authorities were in a difficult position. Should they relax the rigid working practices, backed by the Trade Unions, which excluded women from skilled employment?

SOURCE 12
A poster used for recruiting women into the munitions factories.

'Barclay and Co. in their different branches, now employ about 250 and will by and by employ 500 more. At their head office in Lombard Street a whole floor is now set apart for them. They are now able to use the adding machines. Formerly, to work these required, at every line, a strong pull of a handle, beyond a woman's strength. Now the motive power is supplied by an electric current.'

SOURCE 13
An extract from Reverend Clark's diary from 1915, describing women workers in banks.

'Saturday, 13th November. Mr James Caldwell called. He had talked with a foreman, who said the women-workers were doing splendidly. Lads were often selfishly thoughtless, and larked about. The women worked thoughtfully and steadily.'

SOURCE 14
Another extract from Reverend Clark's diary from 13 November, 1915.

Factory work

From 1915, women were recruited into the factories which produced armaments for the front, see Source 12. They were always paid lower wages than men. Women began to value their new independence and became more assertive. These new roles and new demands sometimes led to resentment and discrimination.

Women took over a range of jobs which had previously been done by men. Hard work and the introduction of new technology meant that production levels were maintained and even increased, see Source 13. Gradually, women won the respect of men, as Source 14 reveals.

attainment target 1

1 What jobs did women do in the war which they had not done before?

2 How did attitudes towards women change after 1915?

3 How did women's jobs change, in offices, in factories and on farms? Which showed the biggest change?

4 Did women like the change brought about by war?

5 Women contributed a great deal to the war effort. How did the changes at work affect changes in other parts of their lives?

ON THE HOME FRONT

Farms

All over Europe, women were also needed on the farms. Many men thought that farm work was 'too hard' for women, but as men were recruited to the army, so they had to be replaced, as Source 15 explains. In Britain, over 260,000 women joined the Women's Land Army. As well as providing food supplies, they helped to break down some of the barriers which had isolated small rural communities.

In both industry and farming, women worked long and hard, see Source 16. Sometimes conditions were hazardous. Women who worked in munitions factories were nicknamed 'canaries' because their hair and skin turned yellow from handling chemicals used for explosives. Shift work was especially difficult for mothers, so the authorities set up pre-school nurseries for their children, see Source 17.

Most women were grateful for the new opportunities that the Great War offered. They felt proud to have contributed to the war effort. Their experience of a more liberated status during the war meant that after 1918 women began new battles for change across a range of social, economic, political and cultural issues.

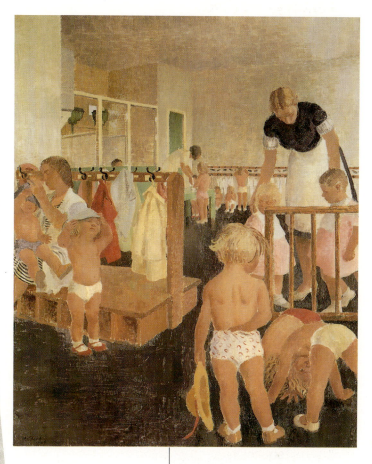

SOURCE 17
This painting by Elsie Hewland shows a nursery school for war workers' children.

'J. Herbert Tritton told me that the War Office had taken nine out of 36 men from his farms; only old men were left. He must get eight women at once, for farm work.'

SOURCE 15
This entry from Reverend Clark's diary is for 19 March 1916.

SOURCE 16
A 'land girl' ploughing, painted by Cecil Aldin.

ON THE HOME FRONT

Families

Source 18 shows one of the most popular soldiers' songs of the Great War. Families in Britain had to 'keep the home fires burning' and, as you can see from Source 19, it was a difficult task.

The contrast in experiences between people serving on the front and people at home often created difficulties when families were re-united during short periods of LEAVE. Families also had to cope with painful goodbyes each time soldiers returned to the front, see Source 20.

Keep the home fires burning
While your hearts are yearning,
Though the lads are far away,
They dream of home.
There's a silver lining,
Through the dark cloud shining,
Turn the dark cloud inside out,
Till the boys come home.

SOURCE 18
'Keep the home fires burning', a popular song from the Great War.

> The average wife and mother . . . had to clothe and feed the children, managing in spite of shortages to make sure that there was enough, or nearly enough, to eat. She had to see that adult members of the family on heavy manual work – which might include herself – had a suitable diet for their jobs. In many parts of the country, she had also to endure air raids, and the drab, colourless life of a nation that had been at war for several years. Yet somehow she had to keep going, binding the family together in the face of general worries and anxieties about the safety of a husband, father or brother away fighting.

SOURCE 19
This extract, written by the historian Stuart Sillars in 1987, describes the pressures which women had to face on the home front.

'The train – hissing insistently, awaiting to ruthlessly tear apart husband and wife, father and child, friend and friend. Such is the ruthlessness of war, individuals cannot be considered . . . . The crowd at the barrier is thinning – sometimes a solitary figure hurries out – having brought to an abrupt conclusion the intensity of the waiting – for a last farewell. Over there stands a young woman clinging to her husband's arms – gazing fixedly at the big white clock, watching, waiting fascinated as the big black minute hand jerks forward, forward!'

SOURCE 20
Elsie Knocker's account of leaving Victoria Station, London, Christmas 1915.

ACTIVITY

You will need to get into mixed sex pairs for this activity. You are going to devise a script for a short role play between a wife and her husband. The wife works shifts, making shells in a large munitions factory. The husband is a Private in the army. He has fought in the trenches for two years. He is home on his first period of home leave.

You should base the conversation around one of these issues:
- Memories of a Zeppelin raid earlier in the year
- Food shortages in the shops
- The death of a mutual friend at the front in a recent trench raid
- The local newspaper's coverage of the war
- Conditions in the trenches.

SOURCE 21
A poster encouraging people to eat less bread, it was issued in 1917.

Shortages and rationing

The dangers which civilians at home had to face partly depended on where they lived and the job they did. Over 8,000,000 civilians died in all countries affected by the Great War. Many families had to cope with hardships and shortages, although the extent of these hardships varied according to social class. Families with status and influence never seemed to suffer the same shortages.

Throughout the war, the government tried to encourage people to economise in the kitchen, see Source 21. In July 1918, the Ministry of Food introduced a system of RATIONING to make sure that food supplies were shared out equally.

Belgium and France

The experiences of civilians living under German occupation close to the front in Belgium and France, offer a stark contrast to the picture in Britain, see Sources 22 and 23. Source 24 describes some of the dangers and difficulties which French civilians living on the Somme had to face.

Vast numbers of civilians were displaced by the war and forced to evacuate their homes. Some families settled in their new surroundings. Others waited to return and reclaim their homes when the war ended. The suffering of thousands of civilians and destruction to the landscape was etched on the French and Belgian national memories for many years after the Great War.

SOURCE 23
A British poster appealing for aid for Belgian civilians.

SOURCE 22
A farmer on the Western Front being watched over by a German soldier.

'Everything was looted, everything. We had to pay them off in gold coins, or they would set fire to the village.'

'One morning they hauled all the 18 to 20 year olds into the square. They took all the young men of the village. They were taken to Germany.'

'My brother should have been taken away. He was 17. As soon as the Germans arrived they took a census. We had to hide him for two years. We were all hungry, because he wasn't counted for the food rations.'

'Here was a semi-front. Trones Wood in the valley was a real front, the trenches, two miles away. You could hear the rifle fire. At night you could see the tracers.'

'We were in a cellar 24 hours a day with German soldiers. Then one day they told us we had to leave. We had two hours. No dawdling.'

SOURCE 24
A transcription of some French women's memories of what life was like during the German occupation of the Somme.

ON THE HOME FRONT

SOURCE 25
'The Surreys play the game': an artist's impression of Captain Nevill leading troops 'over the top'.

Fame and fortune

Today we can follow the exploits of our heroes and heroines by reading newspapers and magazines and watching television. During the Great War, newspapers, magazines and the cinema were also used to create hero figures for the public to admire. It was hard to find heroes amid the mass-fighting of the trenches, so any 'heroic' incidents received wide publicity. Source 25 shows one such incident when Captain Nevill led his troops into action on the Somme by kicking a football 'over the top' into no-man's-land.

In the trenches, soldiers valued the respect of comrades more than any formal recognition of their bravery. 'Rank and file' soldiers were sometimes decorated and they would then be given a hero's welcome from their local community when they returned home on leave. However, it was more usual for officers to receive decorations.

Masters of the field

It was easier for the public to follow senior figures in the army. Picture postcards of them went on sale in Britain. They were photographed in dignified poses, bedecked with their medals, see Source 26.

In France, the careers of certain generals, particularly General Pétain and General Nivelle, were followed closely by the public. After successful campaigns, when morale was running high, these generals became public idols and enjoyed national popularity.

SOURCE 26
A Great War postcard of Sir Douglas Haig.

How were the British generals regarded?

British generals, with the exception of Kitchener, lacked much of the personality of their French counterparts and did not share the same level of devotion from troops or civilians. Nevertheless, their efforts were rewarded with peerages, knighthoods and grants. Statues were erected as permanent and public reminders of the most respected British generals, see Source 27. However, as you can see from Source 28, the memories of many war veterans contrast with the heroic images which were created for the public. You can find out more about attitudes to the British generals on pages 52 to 53.

> 1 What makes a hero? Why did certain men and women become heroic figures of the Great War? What qualities did they have?

ON THE HOME FRONT

SOURCE 27
This statue of Sir Douglas Haig was erected at Whitehall in London in 1937.

'The biggest murderer of the lot was Haig. I'm very bitter, always have been and always will be, and everybody else will that knew him. He lived almost 50 kilometres behind the line and that's about as near as ever he got. I don't think he knew what a trench was like. And they made him an Earl and gave him £100,000 . . . I know what I'd have given him. . . .'

SOURCE 28
Fred Pearson, a Great War veteran, remembers Haig.

'Air aces'

Once the air war started, the media seized the opportunity to make heroes of the most successful fighter pilots. The press eagerly reported each 'kill' that these so called 'air aces' made. In Britain, the most heroic figures were those men who destroyed approaching Zeppelins, see Source 29. In Germany, the public focused their attention on the fighter pilot Baron Manfred von Richthofen, see Source 30. He shot down 80 Allied aircraft in his brief career. He was killed in 1918 at the age of 26. Many fighter pilots on both sides suffered the same fate as Richthofen. All too often, hero worship turned to public grief.

attainment target 2

1 Is Source 28 a statement of fact or opinion?

2 Captain Nevill, in Source 25, is portrayed as a hero. What else would you want to know about this incident before accepting this interpretation?

3 From what you have learned about the Great War so far, do you think Sir Douglas Haig (Sources 26 and 27) was a hero, or do you agree with Fred Pearson? (See Source 28.)

SOURCE 29
The first Zeppelin to be destroyed over Britain was shot down on 3 September 1916.

SOURCE 30
Manfred von Richthofen was known as 'The Red Baron'.

ON THE HOME FRONT

Fighting for peace

As we have seen, the Great War produced a wave of propaganda designed to keep the tide of public opinion in support of the war effort. However, there were people who made a determined effort to swim against this tide. In every warring country, a sizeable minority of people believed that fighting the war was wrong and they had the courage to voice their opinions.

In Britain, men who refused to fight on moral grounds were known as conscientious objectors. In all, 16,000 men were classified as objectors of different degrees. Many were willing to join the army, but not to fight. They went to the Western Front and often had to do dangerous work as stretcher bearers or ambulance drivers. Some of them were treated badly. 'Conchies' who refused to go to the front were sentenced to imprisonment and were also mistreated. Source 31 shows a group of 'conchies' from Dartmoor prison working on the moors.

SOURCE 31
'Conchies' working on Dartmoor.

Peace campaigns

Anti-war protests took place all over Europe. Despite the difficulties of public protest, campaigns to stop the war were organised as early as 1915. A major Women's Peace Conference was held in The Hague in Holland in 1915, see Source 32. Over 1,000 women took part from 12 countries. There were representatives from Germany, Austria, Belgium and Britain as well as from neutral countries. Chrystal Macmillan was one of only three women whom the British Government allowed to attend the meeting. She was also one of the delegates elected to visit the leaders of 35 countries and present them with the Conference peace proposals.

In Britain, The Women's Peace Crusade protested against the fighting by holding meetings, distributing leaflets, and making house to house calls. As Source 33 shows, some soldiers' wives and mothers supported the work of the Crusade.

The authorities and media were hostile to the activities of such organisations. Demonstrations were banned or broken up by people who thought pacifism was unpatriotic during wartime.

---

1 Write a sentence to explain the following terms:
- Anti-war
- Pacifist
- Conscientious objector.

2 Look at Source 22 on page 56 and compare it with Source 32 on this page.
- What are the similarities?
- What are the differences?

3 Why do you think the Hague Conference found it difficult to gain influence?

4 Was the Women's Peace Crusade being unpatriotic in wanting the war to end?

5 Look at Source 35. What objections does Sassoon raise against the Great War?

6 Do you think Sassoon was unpatriotic, a pacifist, a conscientious objector or a coward when he refused to continue his military duties?

7 Why was the USA well placed to put forward plans for peace?

ON THE HOME FRONT

SOURCE 32
The Women's Peace Conference, held at The Hague in 1915.

'One woman, enclosing £10, says, "I have lost one son in the war, another is in the trenches. Thank God that at last the women are waking up".... Four soldiers' wives clubbed together to send 10 shillings, saying they have not known peace of mind since the ghastly slaughter started.'

SOURCE 33
Extracts from *The Labour Leader*, 5 July 1917.

SOURCE 34
Siegfried Sassoon, painted in 1917.

Siegfried Sassoon

The soldier-poet, Siegfried Sassoon, was determined to publicise his objections to the war. His poetry, written while he was serving as an officer at the front, exposed the horror and futility of warfare. In 1917, while he was recovering from wounds, Sassoon decided to make a protest against the continued fighting by refusing to undertake further military duties, see Source 34. He issued a statement to the Army authorities and the press, see Source 35. Sassoon was declared as SHELL-SHOCKED by the authorities and sent to hospital for psychiatric treatment. Later, he returned to the front to prove that his opposition to the war was not based on cowardice.

Attempts to bring peace

Despite their courageous actions, individuals and groups had little influence on the governments of the main enemy nations. Woodrow Wilson, as President of neutral USA, tried to assist in the difficult process of bringing about 'peace without victory'. However, by 1916, both sides felt they had invested too much in gaining victory to settle for any kind of 'compromise' peace. Leaders from both sides were convinced that they could still break the deadlock and win the war. As Source 36 suggests, it was difficult for either side to be seen to be trying to find a compromise solution.

I am making this statement as an act of wilful defiance of military authority, because I believe that the War is being deliberately prolonged by those who have the power to end it. I am a soldier, convinced that I am acting on behalf of soldiers. I believe that this War, upon which I entered as a war of defence and liberation, has now become a war of aggression and conquest. . . . I have seen and endured the sufferings of the troops, and I can no longer be a party to prolonging those sufferings for ends which I believe to be evil and unjust.

SOURCE 35
Extracts from the statement which Siegfried Sassoon made to the authorities in June 1917.

'It was necessary to rouse public opinion in order to fight the war; and this opinion then made it essential to keep the war going. In every country the rulers feared the consequences of ending the war more than they feared the consequences of continuing it.'

SOURCE 36
The historian A.J.P. Taylor made this assessment in 1963.

UNIT 4

AIMS

In this unit we will look at the **Western Front** OFFENSIVES **of 1916 and 1917**. Efforts to end the war brought only costly failures. We shall see how these failures changed attitudes among the troops. We will then look at the impact of trench warfare on civilian life and how the Western Front offensives were reported to the civilians.

On the battle front

Source 1 is a French artist's vision of the Battle of Verdun. This 11 month battle which began in February 1916 has been called the 'worst' in history. The German plan was simple. They wanted 'to bleed France white' by sucking its best troops into defending the fortress city of Verdun. The German artillery would then inflict heavy casualties by massed attacks on a narrow front.

Source 2 shows that Verdun was protected by a ring of forts, but their fire power and troops had been badly run down by 1916. The French knew that if Verdun, a symbol of their military power, fell to the Germans, then the road to Paris would be open to the enemy. The Germans were right: the French were willing to defend the city to the last.

The battle turned into a trial of strength with both sides throwing ever more troops into combat. It is estimated that in total there were 377,000 French losses and 337,000 German losses. Source 3 describes how troops reacted to the horrors of battle. The French, led by General Philippe Pétain, were determined to hold onto Verdun. The stirring order, '*ils ne passeront pas*' (they shall not pass), was issued to the troops.

SOURCE 1
This painting of the Battle of Verdun by Georges Leroux is called 'Hell'.

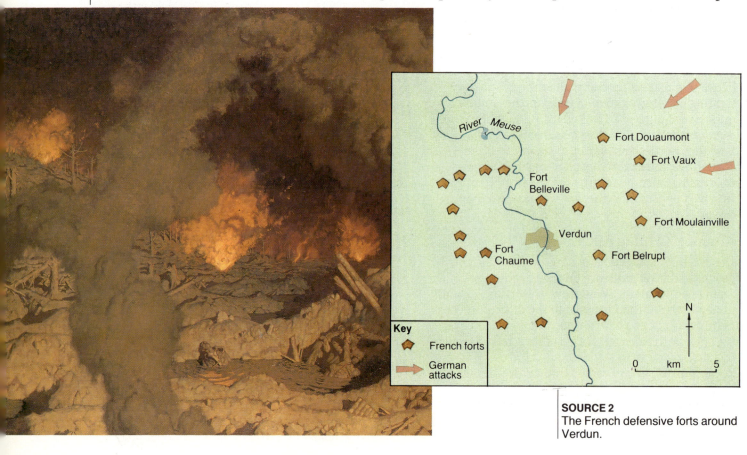

SOURCE 2
The French defensive forts around Verdun.

'The most solid nerves cannot resist for long; the blood mounts to the head; fever burns the body, the nerves, exhausted, become incapable of reaction.'

SOURCE 3
This extract was written by Paul Dubrulle, an infantry sergeant in the Battle of Verdun.

SOURCE 4
This cartoon by Louis Raemakers shows Crown Prince Wilhelm, who led German forces at Verdun, standing on a pile of dead German soldiers and saying 'We must have a higher pile to see Verdun'.

'The ghosts abound . . . it is one of the eeriest places in this world. Everywhere in the spooky jungles the debris of battle still lie, the helmets, the rusted water-bottles, the broken rifles, the huge shell fragments – and, still, the bones.'

SOURCE 6
An extract from *Price of Glory*, an account of the Battle of Verdun, written in 1962.

1. Look at Sources 1 and 3. Which one do you think best presents the horror of Verdun?
2. List the primary and secondary sources used on these pages. Which one do you think has the most impact? Give reasons for your answer.
3. If you were writing about Verdun, do you think it would be more important to present accurate facts or to convey impressions of the battle?
4. Why do you think Verdun is seen as only a short-term victory for the French? What were the long-term results of victory at Verdun?

SOURCE 5
The ossuary of Verdun which was built in the form of a huge shell. It contains the bones of 130,000 dead and is surrounded by a cemetery with 15,000 graves. Building work started in 1923 and the ossuary was completed in 1932.

Bombardment and endurance

The French forts around Verdun withstood colossal bombardment from the German guns. Yet they proved very difficult to capture. In the 11 months of fighting only two major forts fell into German hands. One of these was Fort Vaux where French troops fought to the last, releasing frantic messages for help, until their water supply ran out.

As the battle wore on, both sides grew weary. The German strategy of ATTRITION had not succeeded, see Source 4. German troops had suffered heavy losses and their leaders knew that they themselves had been 'bled white' by Verdun. By the time the French counter-attack was mounted, the Germans had given up hope of capturing Verdun. The exhausted French troops desperately looked to their allies to attack the Germans elsewhere on the Western Front.

The legacy of Verdun

The French claimed Verdun as an 'epic victory'. In the short term it was a victory, but the memory of Verdun scarred deeply into the minds of the French.

A massive OSSUARY was built on the battlefield, see Source 5. The success of the forts in defending Verdun was remembered long after the Great War. A huge network of defensive forts was built all along the French border to protect it from German attack. However, in 1940 they were to prove useless as they were by-passed by a new form of mobile warfare. Around Verdun itself, even today, an atmosphere of violence is still felt by many who visit, see Source 6.

ON THE BATTLE FRONT

Fields in France

As 1 July 1916 dawned in northern France, an early mist gave way to a hot and cloudless midsummer day. Moments before ZERO HOUR at 7.30 am the guns fell silent. Along a 29 kilometre front 100,000 Allied troops waited to attack. The area of gently rolling fields around the River Somme had been a quiet sector of the Western Front until this long-planned offensive was mounted. In the week before 1 July, 1,500 Allied guns had pounded the German positions.

The Allies were confident that nothing would survive the bombardment. Hopes were high, especially among the vast numbers of new recruits who had recently joined up as 'Kitchener's Army'. The tactics of the Allied plan are shown in Source 7.

SOURCE 8
Men advance across no-man's-land at the start of the infantry attack on 1 July 1916.

SOURCE 7
The Allies' plan to break through on the Somme.

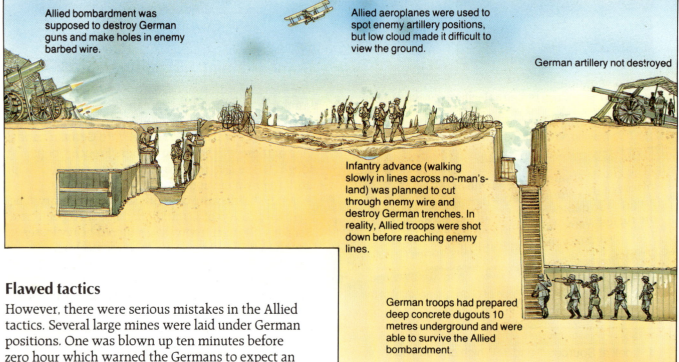

- Allied bombardment was supposed to destroy German guns and make holes in enemy barbed wire.
- Allied aeroplanes were used to spot enemy artillery positions, but low cloud made it difficult to view the ground.
- German artillery not destroyed
- Infantry advance (walking slowly in lines across no-man's-land) was planned to cut through enemy wire and destroy German trenches. In reality, Allied troops were shot down before reaching enemy lines.
- German troops had prepared deep concrete dugouts 10 metres underground and were able to survive the Allied bombardment.

Flawed tactics

However, there were serious mistakes in the Allied tactics. Several large mines were laid under German positions. One was blown up ten minutes before zero hour which warned the Germans to expect an attack. For months the Germans had practised getting men and weapons out from their deep dugouts and into front-line positions. It took them only three minutes. In contrast, the Allied troops were heavily-laden and made slow progress across no-man's-land at a rate of 50 paces per minute. At 7.30 am the infantry advanced. Source 8 shows men crossing no-man's-land and attacking the German lines. The Allied troops were relying upon the German barbed wire being cut, so they could quickly enter the German trenches. However, large sections of it had remained intact, despite the bombardment.

1 Discuss Source 7 in pairs. Decide upon the vital things needed for success on the Somme.

2 Now look at Source 8. What problems can you see for the troops? Using your answers to question 1, list the things which the troops would be expecting ahead and the unexpected things which they would have to face.

ON THE BATTLE FRONT

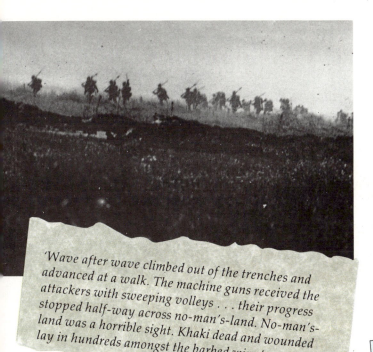

Burial details from Y Ravine cemetery					
Date killed (1916)	Rank		Nationality		Average age when killed
	Officers	Men	British	Canadian	
1 July	2	145	101	46	25
13 November	3	142	145	—	23

Number of unknown graves 143
Total number of graves 432

SOURCE 11
Burial details from the Y Ravine cemetery, built on no-man's-land near Beaumont Hamel in 1917.

'Wave after wave climbed out of the trenches and advanced at a walk. The machine guns received the attackers with sweeping volleys . . . their progress stopped half-way across no-man's-land. No-man's-land was a horrible sight. Khaki dead and wounded lay in hundreds amongst the barbed wire.'

SOURCE 9
A German account of the Allied attack on Beaumont Hamel.

'I still think a lot about the Battle of the Somme. I go through it over and over again. I still do. Those memories are still locked in there. I'll carry them to the grave no doubt. You can't take them away.'

SOURCE 12
Alf Razzle, a 97-year-old war veteran, remembers the Battle of the Somme.

'As soon as the signal for the advance was given . . . machine-gun fire opened up on us. Heaviest casualties occurred on passing through the gaps in our own wire where the men were mown down in heaps.'

SOURCE 10
Part of an entry for 1 July 1916 from the war diary of the Newfoundland Regiment.

Beaumont Hamel

Beaumont Hamel was one of a number of small French villages which the Allied attack was designed to capture from the enemy. Sources 9 and 10 describe the attack on Beaumont Hamel in which 5,240 Allied troops were killed. The Allies gained no ground overall on the first day of the Somme, and lost 29,000 troops. Despite this disastrous beginning the offensive was kept up. Elsewhere some ground was gained, but no breakthrough was achieved. Beaumont Hamel was finally captured by the Allies three and a half months later when a mixture of November fog and poison gas helped a second attack. Even this 'success' involved the loss of 2,200 troops. It was only then that the dead from both attacks could be properly buried.

The battle of the Somme changed the landscape of these French fields. Dotted everywhere, as at Y Ravine near Beaumont Hamel, see Source 11, are hundreds of British cemeteries. They bear witness to an offensive which cost 1,250,000 lives. Its futility hit the British troops very hard, as Source 12 shows. Feelings like those expressed in Source 12 would not go down well back in Britain. How could this disaster be presented to the British public?

1. You will need the trench map Copymaster in the Teacher's Notes for this question. On the trench map, work out, roughly, where the events mentioned in Sources 9 and 10 would have happened.

2. How useful do you think trench maps were in planning an attack?

3. Divide into small groups to discuss all the sources on these two pages. Were the problems in the Allied tactics so serious that the attack was bound to fail? Did the Allies think their attack would fail? Was it wrong to start the attack? Was it wrong to continue?

4. The cemetery register from the Y Ravine cemetery could be used as evidence for an historical investigation. Make a list of questions which you might be able to answer using the register.

ON THE BATTLE FRONT

SOURCE 13
A film still from 'The Battle of the Somme', showing troops advancing across no-man's-land.

a 'Along the entire front the munition dumps are receiving vast supplies of shells; thanks to British munition workers.'

b 'Stretcher cases for ambulance. Wounded awaiting attention at Minden Post. Showing how quickly the wounded are attended to.'

c 'Royal Field Artillery moving up during battle over ground where the Gordons' and Devons' dead are lying after a glorious and successful charge on the ridge near Mametz.'

SOURCE 16
Some of the captions which were used in the film.

'This battle film is really wonderful, a most realistic production but . . . the battle is fought in silence, and the most unpleasant part – the machine gun and rifle fire – is eliminated . . . but on this occasion the roar of the real battle was loud . . . in the distance.'

SOURCE 14
An extract from a letter from Rowland Fielding, Commanding Officer, to his wife.

In years to come, when historians want to know what the conditions were under which the great offensive was launched, they will only have to send for these films and a complete idea of the situation will be revealed before their eyes.

SOURCE 15
A review of the film which appeared in *The Times*, 11 August 1916.

Film, fears and feelings

In September 1916, Lieutenant-Colonel Rowland Fielding was among British troops on the Somme watching an official film of the battle. The 'cinema' was just a screen erected outdoors in a muddy field. Source 13 is taken from the film and Source 14 shows the dramatic impression which the film made on Fielding.

The film, entitled 'The Battle of the Somme, 1916', was made over several days by two cine-cameramen and each of its sections was introduced by a short caption. Eight weeks after the battle started, the film was being shown to audiences throughout Britain and received enthusiastic reviews, see Source 15.

Images of war

The film contains powerful images of trench warfare, but there is no sound, the enemy is not shown and there is no real front line action. Although the film was hailed as an authentic account of events by the media, some sequences were in fact filmed before the battle started, at an army training school. The picture in Source 13 is from one of these 'faked' sequences. Even the captions used in the film were carefully worded to give a positive message, see Source 16.

ON THE BATTLE FRONT

> 'The group helped each carry the guilt of killing, eased the fear ... and gave such security as was possible. It gave mutual support. United by a common jargon, by shared secrets, experiences, discomforts, deep fears, sudden violences and long stillnesses men belonged to platoon or section as to no other aspect of their war life.'

SOURCE 17
An account of the shared experiences of the soldiers. It was written in 1978 by a modern historian.

> 'I gave the men a good look. They seemed in a trance. Their eyes were glassy, their faces white as chalk.... One or two shook hands. An old private, lying down by a young corporal kissed him on the cheek ... I noticed the beads of sweat all over his face.'

SOURCE 18
An extract from the letters of an officer which were published in 1930.

SOURCE 19
Troops in a communication trench at the Battle of the Somme, 1916.

Ere the sun swings his noonday sword
(I) Must say goodbye to all of this;
By all delights that I shall miss,
Help me to die, O Lord.

SOURCE 20
From 'Before Action' written by Lieutenant William Hodgson of the 9th Devonshire Regiment.

Image versus reality

The film did not show the attack for what it was – the greatest single disaster in British military history, with its horrific casualty figures, its lack of land gained, its suicidal tactics. Nor did the film's portrayal of the soldiers reveal the feelings of men about to face battle. Soldiers who fought on the Somme often joined up in groups from the same closely-knit rural communities, or from the same firms, trades and clubs in urban areas. Volunteers in these so-called 'pals' battalions' were promised that they would be able to serve together. In reality they often died together too. The community spirit which developed in the trenches is described in Source 17.

To get a truer picture of the soldiers' feelings, we must go to first-hand accounts. Source 18, for example, shows the unbearable tension felt by soldiers in the zero hour before battle. The photograph in Source 19 was taken of soldiers in their trench just before an attack. Some men even predicted their own deaths. Lieutenant Hodgson of the Devonshire Regiment expressed this in the form of a poem, see Source 20. He was indeed killed moments after zero hour. He was buried with other members of his regiment in a small cemetery on the site of the front line trench. At the entrance to the cemetery, an inscription reads 'The Devonshires held this trench: the Devonshires hold it still'.

attainment target 3

1. Look at Source 16 carefully. What message is each caption designed to give to the home audience?
2. Compare Source 16 (c) with Sources 18 and 20. Do the comments in Source 16(c) seem accurate?
3. Study Source 13. What points would you make to argue that the scene was
   a real, or
   b a fake?
4. Look at Sources 13 and 14. Does the fact that some of the scenes are faked make the claims in Source 15 untrue?

Families and funerals

The Great War was bloodier by far than any other in living memory, as the figures in Source 21 show. Casualties were so high that few families were spared the grief of bereavement, especially after the mass offensives of 1916 to 1918. Today the most obvious reminders of these casualties in Britain are war memorials and Remembrance Day which is commemorated each November, see Source 22.

Figures like those in Source 21 can only tell us the huge numbers that died. To understand the impact these casualties had at the time, we need to think about how the loss of an individual affected those who survived. First would come a War Office telegram. Often this would be followed by a letter from the Commanding Officer and finally the dead soldier's personal belongings. Another way of learning the dreaded news was through lists of men killed which were printed in the newspapers. In Source 23 you can read how Harry Lauder, a music-hall comedian, described his feelings on hearing news of his son's death.

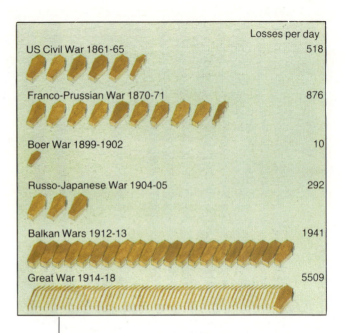

SOURCE 21
Average number of deaths per day in major wars from 1860 until the Great War.

War	Losses per day
US Civil War 1861-65	518
Franco-Prussian War 1870-71	876
Boer War 1899-1902	10
Russo-Japanese War 1904-05	292
Balkan Wars 1912-13	1941
Great War 1914-18	5509

Personal and official accounts

Bereaved families might also receive letters of comfort from friends of the dead soldier. Sometimes soldiers about to face battle wrote moving farewell letters to their loved ones. The soldiers knew that if they were killed, the letters would eventually reach their families and friends when their personal belongings were returned to Britain.

Relatives were given very few official details about a soldier's death. They were usually told that the victim had been killed 'instantaneously' and 'without pain'. However, troops serving with those who died knew differently. The bitter contrast between the reports sent to families and the reality witnessed by fellow soldiers was exposed by Siegfried Sassoon, see Source 24.

SOURCE 22
A Remembrance Day service at the Cenotaph, Whitehall in London.

'I sat and stared at that slip of paper. I had looked upon my boy for the last time. I was quite numb. Then came a great pain... I whispered... the one terrible word "dead". For me... there would be no future. Everything had been swept away by... the hand of fate. I was beyond the power of human words to comfort.'

SOURCE 23
Harry Lauder's reactions to his son's death, written 1 January 1917.

'Jack fell as he'd have wished,' the Mother said,
And folded up the letter that she'd read.
'The Colonel writes so nicely.' Something broke
In the tired voice that quavered to a choke.
She looked up. 'We mothers are so proud
Of our dead soldiers.' Then her face was bowed.

Quietly the Brother Officer went out.
He'd told the poor old dear some gallant lies
That she would nourish all her days, no doubt.
For while he coughed and mumbled, her weak
  eyes
Had shone with gentle triumph, brimmed with
  joy,
Because he'd been so brave, her glorious boy.

He thought how 'Jack', cold-footed, useless
  swine,
Had panicked down the trench that night the
  mine
Went up at Wicked Corner; how he'd tried
To get sent home, and how, at last, he died,
Blown to small bits. And no one seemed to care
Except that lonely woman with white hair.

SOURCE 24
Siegfried Sassoon's poem, 'The Hero', written in 1916.

Communities in mourning

One in nine British soldiers never came home. Within small or tightly-knit communities, the impact of these casualties was marked. Signs of families in mourning – lowered window blinds and black clothing – were common everywhere. News of the heavy Somme casualties were deliberately 'drip fed' by the authorities into the newspaper columns from late August until late October 1916. But censorship could not conceal the true extent of the casualties nor, as Source 25 emphasises, their long-term results.

Burying the dead

Casualties were so heavy that the army decided to bury British and Empire troops where they fell rather than returning them home, see Source 26. If the body was identified, the family could choose their own inscription for a grave, but at their expense. However, after the mass offensives of 1916 to 1918 half the dead were unidentified. Families of these soldiers could only be told that they were 'missing, presumed dead' and that there was 'no known grave'. Vast memorials listing the names of these soldiers were built on the Somme and at Ypres.

'I can remember my mother getting that telegram that evening as she was bathing us for bed. She collapsed on the floor. We helped her into a chair and she told us Daddy was missing. . . . It ruined us for the rest of our lives, because my father had a good job and we were just left with mother having to struggle, we had to do without lots of things other children had.'

SOURCE 25
A woman remembers hearing the news of her father's death. This is a transcription of an oral testimony.

SOURCE 26
Bodies of Australian soldiers awaiting burial near Guillemont on the Somme, 1918.

ACTIVITY

1. In pairs, consider the argument for or against the British decision that 'the dead should rest with the main body of their comrades'. If you were a relative of a dead soldier, what would you want?

2. Find out if your local area, or your school, has a war memorial or plaque for those killed in the Great War.

3. Make a study of the memorial. You could organise your findings under these headings: location, data, appearance and function.

4. You could investigate its origins by finding out when it was built, who had it built, how much it cost and when it was first unveiled. Articles in local newspapers, parish or school magazines and oral accounts from elderly people could help.

ON THE BATTLE FRONT

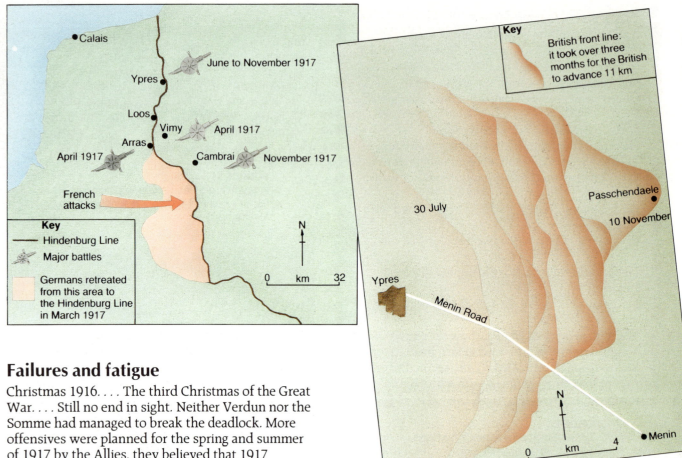

SOURCE 27
The 1917 offensives on the Western Front. The inset shows the Flanders offensive.

Failures and fatigue

Christmas 1916.... The third Christmas of the Great War.... Still no end in sight. Neither Verdun nor the Somme had managed to break the deadlock. More offensives were planned for the spring and summer of 1917 by the Allies, they believed that 1917 would be the year in which Germany would finally be defeated. For a brief moment, in March, it seemed that the Allies might have been right.

The Germans found out about French and British attacks to come and withdrew to their long-prepared fortified defensive zone called the 'Hindenburg Line' (see Source 27). The deadlock became harder than ever to break. All the troops were battle-weary and because of this the various Allied offensives ended in unexpected ways.

The French mutiny

Failure was just too much for some of the French troops, see Source 28. About 30,000 men deserted from duty. Some regiments even mutinied – they disobeyed orders and refused to fight. The mutinies were followed by strikes and riots which spread across France. The French government turned to General Pétain, the 'Saviour of Verdun', to restore order. The ring-leaders of the mutiny were shot, but the French army had been badly shaken and it took time for the troops to recover from their low morale. In the meantime, any other major attacks on the Western Front would have to be mounted by British and Empire troops.

SOURCE 28
A lithograph which shows French soldiers in rebellious mood.

Desertion on the Eastern Front

Troops from the Russian army serving on the Eastern Front also deserted after mounting an offensive which failed, see Source 29. But they had other motives too. Russia's troops had suffered three years of shortages and supply problems, along with too many defeats and retreats. The Tsar had left the throne and war-weary troops responded to new calls for peace from the Bolsheviks following the Russian revolution. Against its new government's wishes, thousands of Russian soldiers fled the war-zone and returned home. Russia no longer supported Britain and France as their ally and made peace with Germany.

Italy had begun the Great War as Germany's ally but it soon withdrew to a position of neutrality. In 1917 Italian troops fought a series of battles against Austrian forces and they suffered a severe defeat. This also made matters worse for the Allies.

SOURCE 29
Russian soldiers deserting from the Eastern Front in 1917.

Flanders fields

The place chosen for the main British offensive of 1917 was Flanders, in Belgium. Despite its low-lying land, the wet Autumn weather and the strongly defended German positions, General Haig thought that it would be possible to break through the German lines. Today it is an area of peaceful farms, villages and small towns. But the names of some of its settlements recall the full horror of the Great War, and none more so than Passchendaele. It was here that the exhausted Allies stopped. Only 11 kilometres of mud and shell holes were gained, see Source 30, at a cost of over 500,000 lives from both sides. Haig tried to justify his tactics of attrition as being used to wear down the enemy to breaking point. But the horrors were shared equally by all who fought in Flanders.

The Flanders offensive of 1917 has been called 'the battle of the mud'. 'Passchendaele' is no longer just part of an historical event. It has become a powerful symbol of the Great War in being the 'blindest slaughter of a blind war'.

SOURCE 30
The devastated landscape of Flanders, 1917.

attainment target 1

1. Look at Source 30. The items labelled 1, 2 and 3 can be linked as causes and effects. Explain these links.
2. Why did the Allied offensives on all fronts fail in 1917? Here are some possible causes: War weary troops; loss of morale; bad generals; strength of German defences; bad government at home; failures of 1914 to 1916; 20th century weaponry; attacks in the wrong places.
   a. Choose two which you think help to explain the French mutiny.
   b. Choose two which you think help to explain desertions on the Russian front.
   Explain your answers in each case.
3. Choose a short-term and a long-term cause of the British failure at Passchendaele. Explain your choice.
4. Which do you think was the most important single reason for the British failure at Passchendaele? Compare your choice with two other causes which you think were less important.

ON THE BATTLE FRONT

Fatalism

There was no Christmas truce in 1917: the British generals were afraid that it would weaken the offensive spirit of the troops. However, by this time the troops facing each other across no-man's-land felt more in sympathy with each other than ever, see Source 31. Indeed they had other 'enemies' in common – their own leaders, profiteers back at home who were doing well out of the war, the politicians – in short all who were keen to continue the war.

After the slaughter of 1916 and 1917, many soldiers lost the optimism and enthusiasm which had been so strong among many of them when the war started. They were now only concerned with survival, as Source 32 makes clear. Every soldier knew that 'attrition' meant being wounded or killed sooner or later. General Haig admitted the change in attitude among his troops, see Source 33.

'July 1916. I am enjoying life hugely. I love the army – and it is a great game.'

'August 1916. I hate all this business from the bottom of my soul. All this area is one vast cemetery. Dead bodies taint the air wherever you go. It has robbed thousands ... of the things that made life seem worth living.'

SOURCE 32
Extracts from two letters sent home by Edward Chapman of the Royal Fusiliers.

'The man in the ranks is no longer aware of why he is fighting. He has lost both faith and enthusiasm.'

SOURCE 33
An extract from the diaries of General Haig, 1918.

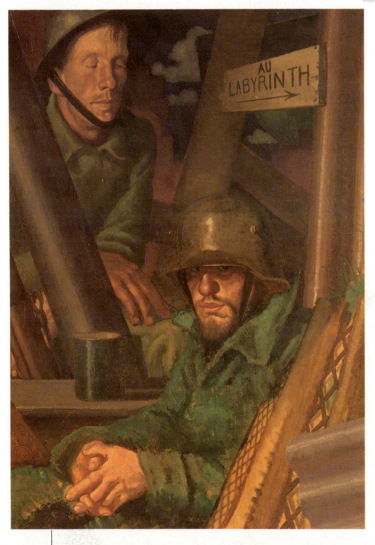

SOURCE 31
A British soldier guards a captured German.

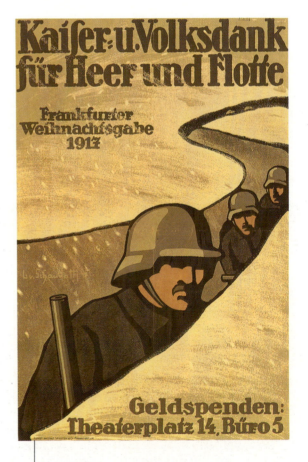

SOURCE 34
A German poster appealing for donations from Christmas 1917. It says 'The Kaiser and the people thank the army and the fleet'.

ON THE BATTLE FRONT

Conscription

Heavy losses in the early stages of the war forced the British Government to introduce CONSCRIPTION in 1916. At first only single able-bodied men were called up for military service, but conscription was later extended to married men too. Both France and Germany had long before set up systems of conscription to make up for the casualties they expected to suffer.

In spite of the massive losses, the endurance of all troops was remarkable and civilian support continued, see Sources 34 and 35. No less remarkable was the ability of French and Belgian civilians to carry on with their lives near the front, often under the control of the German forces, see Source 36. All concerned at the front wanted an end to the war as quickly as possible, as Source 37 shows.

'Over and over again it is the duty of men to charge against barbed wire into almost certain death. Often no one comes back. Yet there is never any hesitation or questioning.'

SOURCE 35
Part of a letter written by Rowland Fielding to his wife.

'You cannot imagine the longing of every man in this Army for the end of the war.'

SOURCE 37
A British army officer's diary records the troops' feelings.

SOURCE 36
A ruined village on the Western Front, March 1917.

ON THE BATTLE FRONT

Anger and bitterness

Some troops began to react angrily to their situation. Although there were some breakdowns in discipline, the anger was more often expressed through popular songs like 'I don't want to be a soldier' or through drawings and paintings which exposed the horrors of the fighting. You can read the lyrics from one of the trench songs in Source 38 and Source 39 is a painting by John Nash. For some, anger gave way to bitterness. Wilfred Owen, who was killed one week before the war ended, wrote his bitter poem '*Dulce et Decorum est*' in 1917. You can read an extract from this poem in Source 40.

So there was still deadlock on the Western Front and the troops were suffering from desperation and exhaustion. The war continued to swallow up vast stocks of resources, while at home the impact of shortages was beginning to hit millions of innocent civilians.

I want to go home, I want to go home,
I don't want to go in the trenches no more,
Where whizzbangs and shrapnel they whistle and roar.
Take me over the sea, where the *alleyman* can't get at me;
Oh my, I don't want to die, I want to go home.

alleyman   German (from the French word 'allemand')

SOURCE 38
A popular soldiers' song.

If in some smothering dreams you too could pace
Behind the wagon that we flung him in,
And watch the white eyes writhing in his face,
His hanging face, like a devil's sick of sin;
If you could hear, at every jolt, the blood
Come gargling from the froth-corrupted lungs,
Obscene as cancer, bitter as the cud
Of vile, incurable sores on innocent tongues, –
My friend, you would not tell with such high zest
To children ardent for some desperate glory,
The old Lie: *Dulce et decorum est
Pro patria mori.*

Dulce et decorum est pro patria mori   It is sweet and proper to die for one's country

SOURCE 39
A detail from John Nash's painting 'Over the top'.

SOURCE 40
The closing lines from '*Dulce et Decorum est*' by Wilfred Owen.

attainment target 1

Look at pages 46 to 48 to answer these questions.

1. What does Source 31 suggest to you about enemy soldiers' feelings towards each other and the war?

2. Sort Sources 32 to 40 into two types by drawing the table below and filling it in.

Source number	Type 1: to carry on and 'finish the job'	Type 2: to end the war and its futile fighting

Do your findings show that all soldiers thought the same?

3. The popular image is that all the soldiers were fed up with the war by 1918. From the evidence in Sources 32 to 40 do you agree with this image?

4. Do you think that the infantry really meant the words which they sang like those in Source 38?

5. Is it fair to say that in 1914 everyone wanted war and that by 1918 no one wanted it?

Fleets in danger

With the armies deadlocked on land, both sides turned to the seas to put more pressure on the enemy. Each side wanted to stop the flow of imports which could be used to manufacture weapons and war equipment. They also tried to create shortages of vital foodstuffs so that civilian support for the war effort would weaken.

The Germans mobilised their fleet of submarines to sink Allied merchant ships with torpedoes, see Source 41. The British strategy was to impose a blockade on German ports to prevent the entry of supplies. At first the U-Boat campaign was directed at ships from countries at war with Germany. Then in 1915 a German U-boat sank the British passenger-liner the *Lusitania*. The *Lusitania* was carrying 128 US passengers who were among the 1,198 people who drowned. Neutral USA was angered and dismayed by Germany's actions. By 1917 Germany intensified its campaign of submarine warfare and began to attack ships from any nation bringing supplies to the Allies. Several US ships were sunk. These actions helped to bring the USA into the war in April 1917, see Source 42.

SOURCE 41
'U-Boats Out!' – a German poster designed by Hans Rudi Erdt.

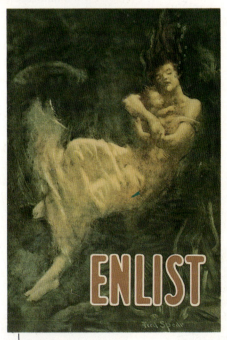

SOURCE 42
An American recruitment poster, recalling the sinking of the *Lusitania* by German U-Boats.

Year	Average number of U-Boats in action each month	Tonnes of British shipping lost
1915	30	762,640
1916	60	898,170
1917	110	3,373,480
1918	115	1,686,620

SOURCE 43
The effects of the German U-Boat campaign.

---

1. Look carefully at Sources 41 and 42. Draw the following table and fill it in to compare the two posters.

Source number	Visual impact	Obvious message	Hidden message

   Think about why the posters were produced and what effect they were intended to have.

2. Now use a similar table to compare one of the posters with a modern magazine advertisement.

Different strategies

By 1917 both sides were experiencing shortages as a result of each other's efforts. The early success of the U-Boat campaign against merchant ships, shown in Source 43, meant that certain items had to be rationed to the public in Britain. Rationing was very unpopular but necessary: food stocks in Britain were down to just six weeks' supplies in the winter of 1917. The situation improved when the Allies introduced a convoy system to protect merchant shipping with warships. Although the deadlock looked set to continue, in the long-term the British naval blockade proved to be a more successful strategy than the German U-Boat campaign.

UNIT 5

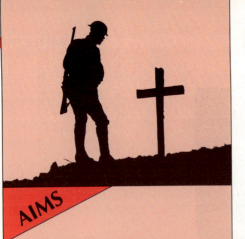

AIMS

In this unit we will see how the war came to an end in 1918. We will then focus on the short-term results of the Great War and how relief soon turned to disenchantment and fear.

We will look at the lasting symbols of the Great War in our landscape and our culture. The unit ends by suggesting how you might make a study of how your local area was affected by the Great War.

The aftermath

At the start of 1918, there was still no end in sight to the deadlock. Yet by the end of the year the Great War was over. What caused such a dramatic turn-around of events? Opinions among historians have varied on the key reasons for the Allied victory. How were these victories achieved? Why were German forces exhausted by the summer of 1918?

Germany decided to launch a final attack on the Western Front, using extra troops who had been freed from fighting the Russians on the Eastern Front. The German leaders feared that if this offensive failed, their weary troops might be overpowered by the American forces coming to join the Allies. Germany had been fighting on two fronts for four years and its resources for the war effort were being rapidly used up, as Source 1 shows. Millions of German civilians were struggling against starvation and disease.

The German attack began in March 1918 and, at first, was successful. German forces punched holes through the Allied lines and forced the Allies to retreat and defend, see Source 2. At one point, Paris itself seemed in danger. Allied casualties escalated and the Germans were poised for victory. Allied leaders issued desperate orders like the one in Source 3. Despite heavy losses, Allied troops held on to their positions.

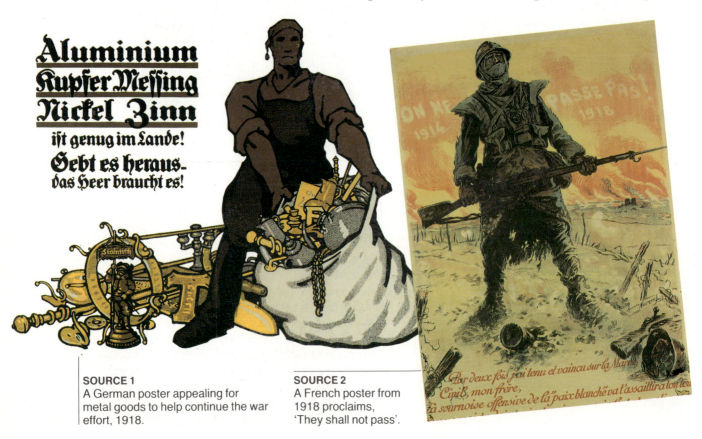

SOURCE 1
A German poster appealing for metal goods to help continue the war effort, 1918.

SOURCE 2
A French poster from 1918 proclaims, 'They shall not pass'.

> Three weeks ago the enemy began terrific attacks against us. . . . Victory will belong to the side which holds out the longest. . . . Every position must be held to the last man: there must be no retirement. With our backs to the wall, and believing in the justice of our cause, each one of us must fight on to the end.

SOURCE 3
The day's order issued by Haig to all ranks, 11 April 1918.

SOURCE 4
A sea of German prisoners, 1918.

Retreat and defeat

By mid-July, the Allies were reinforced with fresh American troops. They halted the German advance and mounted a series of counter-attacks. The German army was exhausted and its short-supplied troops surrendered in vast numbers, see Source 4. By the autumn, the German forces were in retreat along the Western Front. The battlefields of 1915 to 1917 were re-captured by the Allies for the last time.

The Great War, known for its stubborn deadlock, was ending as it began: with a flurry of rapid movement of men and machines. The Allies learned from the experience of various successful opening attacks in 1917, using a combination of improved infantry tactics and new weapons. The British armies bore the brunt of the fighting in the autumn of 1918. They achieved a series of nine victories from August to November which forced Germany to seek an ARMISTICE. Source 5 acknowledges these achievements.

> 'Never at any time in history has the British army achieved greater results in attack. The victory was indeed complete, thanks to the commanders of armies, corps and divisions, thanks above all to the wise, loyal and energetic policy of their Commander-in-Chief.'

SOURCE 5
The Allies' Supreme Commander, Marshal Foch, pays tribute to the British army, 1918.

> 'Runner in at 10.30 am with order to cease firing at 11.00 am. . . . Firing continued. Machine gun company on my right lost 12 men at 10.55, when a high explosive landed in their position. . . . At 11.00 sharp the shelling ceased on both sides. . . . Captain came up and told us that the war was over.'

SOURCE 6
Part of the entry from Sergeant Grady's diary, 11 November 1918.

1 Which argument do you generally support?
- The Allies defeated the German army on the Western Front.
- The German army lost the war as a result of its own actions.
- The German army lost the war as a result of forces beyond its control.

2 Why have the Allied victories of 1918 been given relatively little attention?

3 How does Marshal Foch's view (Source 5) of the British leadership compare with your own earlier opinions?

Armistice

By November, Germany was no longer able to hold on to its own positions or retain its allies. The German people became more interested in food than fighting and leaders turned to face revolutionaries within Germany, instead of the lost cause of continuing the war.

The end came quite suddenly. On 8 November, the Kaiser fled to neutral Holland. News of an armistice filtered through to the troops, but as Source 6 describes, the fighting continued right up until the eleventh hour of the eleventh day of the eleventh month. When the Armistice was officially declared, the millions of survivors were left with feelings of relief and celebration mixed with a sense of loss.

THE AFTERMATH

Followers and fools?

Many people have criticised the leadership of the British generals and in particular, that of the Commander-in-Chief, Sir Douglas Haig. Some people hold the view that the British soldiers of the Great War were 'lions led by donkeys'. As Source 7 shows, these accusations have continued right up to modern times. Others have argued that the British generals have yet to receive credit for achieving victory in 1918.

The charges

In *British Butchers and Bunglers of World War One*, John Laffin accuses the generals of 'bungling' and poor leadership which resulted in the 'butchery' or waste of soldiers' lives on a huge scale. His criticisms are listed in Source 8.

The case against

Many soldiers who survived the war had very bitter memories and blamed the actions of Haig and the generals for the high number of casualties, see Source 9. The war poets added their voices to these criticisms of the leadership, see Source 10.

In the 1920s and 1930s politicians were also critical of the way in which the British war effort had been conducted under the leadership of the British generals. In particular, they were concerned that so many lives had been lost for a very small gain of enemy ground. Politicians accused the generals of sending out British troops to fight in impossible conditions while they themselves enjoyed a comfortable lifestyle detached from the horrors of the trenches. British casualties in the Second World War were less than half those suffered in the Great War. This strengthened the view of historians that the Great War had been mis-managed by uncaring leaders.

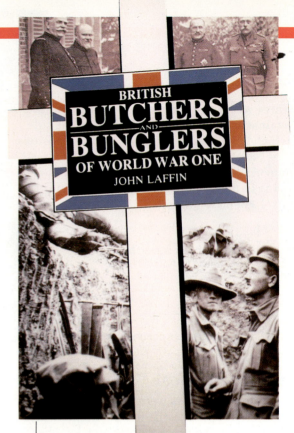

SOURCE 7
John Laffin's attack on the British generals, *British Butchers and Bunglers of World War One*, was published in 1988.

'I think General Haig wanted shooting. He was a man who never cared for men's lives. About 1917 we called him the 'butcher'. I don't know anything about generals – I never had any contact with them.'

SOURCE 9
A veteran of the Great War recalls his memories of General Haig.

- How could the Allied armies lose so many men?
- Why didn't the general public, as well as the press and pulpit, complain?
- Why did the generals persist with the same methods of attack?
- How could generals accept such losses on their own side?
- Did no other strategies exist?
- Did the generals know and understand conditions on the battlefield?
- Did any of these generals have any sense of shame over their failings and the loss of life?

SOURCE 8
From *British Butchers and Bunglers of World War One*.

'Good-morning; good-morning!' the General said
When we met him last week on our way to the line.
Now the soldiers he smiled at are most of 'em dead,
And we're cursing his staff for incompetent swine.
'He's a cheery old card', grunted Harry to Jack
As they slogged up to Arras with rifle and pack.
                    *
But he did for them both by his plan of attack.

SOURCE 10
This poem was written by Sassoon in 1917. He fought in the battle of Arras and was wounded there.

THE AFTERMATH

The case for

The case which supports the conduct of the British generals rests upon the fact that in 1918, the German army was defeated. From the evidence available – letters home and diaries – it seems that during the war, bitterness towards the generals was not widespread in the trenches. The troops made numerous complaints about trench conditions and army life, and they often envied the 'cushy' lifestyle of the generals. But looking back, many soldiers admit that their war experiences were very localised and this prevented them from making wider criticisms. Furthermore, the majority of soldiers never had any contact with the generals.

In Britain, few voices were heard which criticised the handling of the war. Despite the long casualty lists which they printed, newspapers and magazines always presented events in a positive way and did not blame the leadership.

> 'I don't suppose any military men in history have ever had such a 'bad press' as those unfortunate officers who led the British Army to the greatest sequence of victories in its history. I find it very strange. Victory was their duty and they did not fail.'

SOURCE 11
From an article written by John Terraine, 1982.

attainment target 2

1. Give examples of facts and opinions from Sources 8 and 11.
2. Choose two sources from this book which you could use to support John Laffin's accusation that the generals were 'butchers and bunglers'.
3. How does Source 12 support the interpretation in Source 11?
4. Which view of the generals do you agree with – John Laffin's or John Terraine's? Explain your answer.
5. Why, despite achieving victory, have the British generals been so heavily criticised?

After the war

The case for the generals has been argued most strongly by John Terraine, see Source 11. In response to John Laffin's criticisms which are listed in Source 8, Terraine says that the generals of the Great War faced a unique combination of problems, see Source 12. Terraine argues that faced with an enemy of such vast numbers, the British generals had no option but to mount their offensives in 1916 to 1917, and that heavy casualties were to be expected. He claims that the series of Allied victories in 1918 were gained against overwhelming odds and were a remarkable achievement. He argues that Allied leaders deserve more credit than they have been given. He also points out that it was the politicians, not the generals, who had final responsibility for events.

SOURCE 12
This diagram shows the factors which the British generals faced, according to John Terraine.

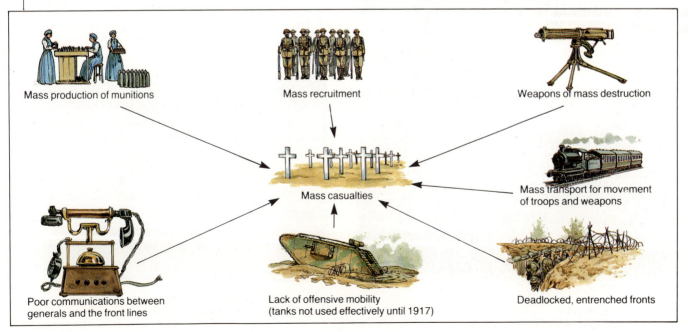

The future for Europe

By 1918, civilians all over Europe were war-weary. They had endured four years of living under the grim shadow of war. They suffered crippling food shortages and, in some cases, starvation, see Source 13. Their clothing, heating and lighting were rationed. They lived under the constant threat of air-raids. They worked tirelessly on the land, in the munitions factories and in the hospitals where they nursed the endless stream of casualties from the front. They had to cope with separation, worry and grief.

In 1918 to 1919, a new strain of the infectious influenza virus, nicknamed 'Spanish Flu' swept across the world, see Sources 14 and 15. Soldiers and civilians, weakened by war, had very low resistance to the virus. It claimed an estimated 27 million lives, more than the number of people who had died in trench warfare during the Great War.

'If one looks at the women worn away to skin and bone and with seamed and careworn faces, one knows where the portion of food assigned to them has really gone.'

SOURCE 13
This description of German women was written at the end of the Great War.

'My dear Miss Mildred,
Excuse me to have been so long in answering your last letter but we have been so busy with the influenza epidemic, that I could do nothing except preparations for my father; this epidemic was terrible especially in Tours and Lyon, terrible also for our poor soldiers; I know by 'Papers' that England did much suffer of it.'

SOURCE 14
This letter, written in December 1918, describes the 'Spanish flu' epidemic in France.

Returning home

At the end of the Great War, British soldiers returned home with high hopes of a more secure future: stable jobs, better housing, increased wages and a higher standard of living. They were promised 'Homes fit for heroes'. However, vast sums of money had been spent financing the war. Industry had been severely disrupted and some valuable overseas markets were lost. It was therefore difficult to fulfil the promises of a brighter future, see Source 16.

SOURCE 15
Spraying a bus with anti-flu liquid.

SOURCE 16
Ex-soldiers working as street hawkers, February 1920.

Women's lives after the war

It was not only the returning soldiers who faced disappointment. Women, who had earned greater independence and respect in wartime, were pushed back into their traditional roles during the 1920s. Many women who had worked for the war effort, found it difficult to get jobs after the war, see Source 17. Source 18 shows that the authorities wanted to return to pre-war working practices which kept many jobs for men only. However, their wartime experiences made women more determined to fight for greater equality with men. In Britain in 1918, women over the age of 30 were given the right to vote and in 1928 this right was extended to women over 21.

Soldiers from the British Empire

Many volunteers from the British Empire had joined up during the Great War, see Source 19. The Indian sub-continent sent over 1,200,000 troops to fight for the Allies. Many of these men hoped that their contribution to the war effort might hasten the process of Indian independence from Britain. However, this was not the case. In 1919, nearly 400 Indians attending a peaceful demonstration were killed by British soldiers. This event, the Amritsar Massacre, showed that British opposition to Indian independence had hardened.

SOURCE 17
Women queuing for work after the war.

'Any rule, practice or custom departed from during the war is to be restored . . . Where new branches have been established within an industry, pre-war practices are to apply to it.'

SOURCE 18
Clauses 1 and 2 from the Restoration of Pre-war Practices Act which was passed in August 1919.

attainment target 1

1. How and why did civilian attitudes to war change between 1914 and 1918? You may need to look back at Unit 1.
2. What social and economic changes did British soldiers hope for when they returned home?
3. How did the lives of British women change at the end of the Great War?
4. Read Source 18. Do you think that the attitude of the authorities towards women changed after the war?
5. Do you agree with the opinion that although women's lives were changed by the Great War, there was not any progress in their position in society?

SOURCE 19
Indian troops using bayonets during a training exercise.

THE AFTERMATH

The future for Germany

At the beginning of 1918, President Woodrow Wilson of the USA offered a 14-point peace plan to end the war. At the time, the Germans rejected the plan. This meant that they were later forced to make an unconditional surrender according to terms laid down by the Allies. The survivors of the defeated German army faced a very uncertain future of economic hardship and political unrest. However, the leaders of the German troops tried to maintain optimism by issuing orders like the one in Source 20.

Civilians in the Allied countries felt that Germany should be called to account for the mass destruction of the war. Slogans such as 'Hang the Kaiser!' and 'Squeeze Germany until the pips squeak!' were used during the British General Election of 1918. Feelings ran equally high in France as you can see from Source 21.

> Undefeated by the enemy we have to abandon the territory we have occupied. We can march back to our country with heads held high. Keep the German Army's honour to the last, and then, in spite of the unhappy end, you will be able to look back full of pride, to the very end of your days, upon your heroic deeds.

SOURCE 20
Orders issued to German units in November 1918.

SOURCE 21
This French poster shows the French leader using bleach to wash away the Kaiser's crimes.

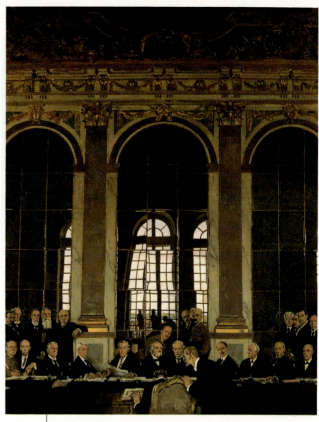

SOURCE 22
The signing of the Treaty of Versailles, 28 June 1919.

> 'When the Treaty of Versailles was published, I deliberately refrained from reading it; I was beginning already to suspect that my generation had been deceived, its young courage exploited, its idealism betrayed.'

SOURCE 23
An extract from Vera Brittain's *Testament of Youth*, which was first published in 1933.

The Treaty of Versailles

The Allied leaders took these public demands that Germany should pay compensation to the Peace Conference held at Versailles in 1919. The conference was dominated by the leaders of the victorious countries. Germany was not allowed to be present during discussions, yet major issues concerning Germany's territory, industry and military strength were discussed. One part of the TREATY which angered the Germans was the 'war guilt' clause. It insisted that Germany was solely responsible for the outbreak of the Great War, and should therefore pay for damage in the form of REPARATIONS to the Allies.

THE AFTERMATH

The Treaty of Versailles was signed in June 1919, see Source 22. The German delegates were faced with a stark choice: to sign away German lands, economic power and military strength or face invasion from Allied forces. The issue of reparations took years to sort out. Eventually, in 1921, a figure of £6,600 million was accepted, to be paid in instalments. The harsh terms laid down by the Allies in the peace treaty created bitterness among the defeated powers. There were also doubts among the British public that the treaty would bring about a stable period of peace as Source 23 shows. Events in the 1930s were to prove that the treaty failed to overcome the serious political issues which split the winners and losers of the Great War.

Anti-war feeling

By the end of the 1920s, the Great War – the 'war to end wars' – seemed futile and the Treaty of Versailles a failure. Anti-war feelings were expressed through a variety of artistic channels, including novels, plays, poetry, paintings, sculptures and films, see Sources 24 to 26. These impressions of futility fuelled public fears of another war in Europe in the 1930s.

SOURCE 24
This picture, which recalls the horrors of the Great War battlefields, was painted by the German artist, Otto Dix.

SOURCE 25
This is a still from the anti-war film 'All Quiet on the Western Front' which was made in 1930.

Look at Sources 24 to 26

1 Why did poems and pictures have a powerful impact on people in the 1920s?

2 What impact do they have on you?

3 Do you think written expressions of anti-war feelings are more powerful than visual ones? Give reasons for your answer.

> I have returned to these:
> The farm, and kindly Bush and the young calves lowing,
> But all that my mind sees,
> Is a quaking bog in a mist – stark, snapped trees,
> And the dark Somme flowing.

SOURCE 26
Part of a poem written by an Australian, Vance Palmer, who fought in the Great War. Like millions of others, he was unable to forget the devastation and misery he had seen in the trenches. He wrote this poem in 1920.

THE AFTERMATH

SOURCE 28
The Royal Artillery Memorial in London.

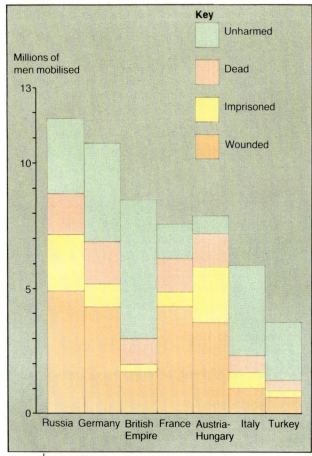

SOURCE 27
The fate of the armies, 1914 to 1918.

SOURCE 29
Memorial to the missing at Thiepval on the Somme.

The Fallen

People across Europe felt the loss of a whole generation, see Source 27. Individuals, communities and entire nations were in mourning. Many memorials to the dead were built in the 1920s, see Source 28. On the Western Front itself, memorials were erected for the vast numbers of unidentified or missing soldiers. You can see one of these memorials in Source 29.

Today, perhaps the most direct reminders of the enormous loss of life are the sprawling cemeteries which now stand on the sites of the Western Front battlefields, see Source 30. Visitors to these cemeteries are often struck by how young the victims were. The preserved forts, trenches and shell craters serve to remind visitors of the intensity of the battles.

THE AFTERMATH

Remembrance

The annual Remembrance Day in November allows the countries who fought in the Great War to focus on the people who were killed. Poppies, which are an emblem of the Great War (Source 31), are worn for Remembrance Day. The Western Front Association was founded in 1980 to ensure that people would not forget the courage and comradeship of soldiers from both sides who had fought in the trenches.

As the 21st century approaches, what is the point of remembering the Great War? Is it still relevant, as Source 32 questions? Or perhaps it is better to forget it, as Source 33 suggests, since the enemies of the Great War are now partners, working to promote co-operation in Europe.

SOURCE 30
The British Y Ravine cemetery at Beaumont Hamel.

'Our plastic throw-away, take-away society is completely alien to the spartan values for which the men of 1914 to 1918 fought and died. What place does "courage", "comradeship", "loyalty" and above all, "sacrifice" have in the "me" world? . . . The bewilderment on the faces of the aged survivors of the war when I asked them what they thought of the modern world, was painful to behold.'

SOURCE 32
An extract from *The War Walk*, written in 1983 by Nigel Jones.

In Flanders fields the poppies blow
Between the crosses, row on row,
That mark our place: and in the sky
The larks, still bravely singing, fly
Scarce heard amid the guns below.

We are the Dead. Short days ago
We lived, felt dawn, saw sunset glow,
Loved and were loved, and now we lie
In Flanders fields.

Take up our quarrel with the foe:
To you from failing hands we throw
The torch; be yours to hold it high.
If ye break faith with us who die
We shall not sleep, though poppies grow
In Flanders fields.

SOURCE 31
'In Flanders Fields', written by John McCrae in 1915. He was a Canadian army doctor stationed near Ypres.

On the hills outside the city, I was held up by roadworks. A bull-dozer was at work, cutting a new road, and as its blade entered the earth out tumbled German steel-helmets of the First World War. It was a strange sensation. Here I was, a German officer on my way to sit in conference with our French allies . . . I could hardly believe that all this had happened only forty-four years ago, even just within my lifetime. It was more like watching archaeologists dig up the very distant past.

SOURCE 33
A German NATO official describes his journey to a conference in Paris which took him past Verdun.

1. Why are poppies used as an emblem of the Great War?
2. Are poppies sold in your school for Remembrance Day? Which charity organises the selling of poppies and how do they use the money which is collected?

THE AFTERMATH

Finding out

It is now over seven decades since the Great War came to an end, but as we have seen, there are still many reminders of the events of 1914 to 1918. How was your local community affected by the Great War?

Sources 34 to 37 relate to the small industrial town of Birtley in north east England. In 1916, the National Projectile Factory opened in Birtley. It supplied artillery shells to the British troops, see Source 35. Today, the same building houses the Royal Ordnance Factory designing high-tech shells and making rocket motors.

Elisabethville

A settlement for about 5,000 Belgian refugees was set up in Birtley, see Source 36. It was called Elisabethville. As well as huts for the refugees, there were also shops, schools, communal dining rooms, a hospital, church and laundry. The streets were named after members of the Belgian royal family and some of these street names still exist in the area today. Although many of the refugees returned to Belgium after the war, some of them died and were buried in Birtley. Graves of 13 Belgians can be found in Birtley cemetery today, see Source 37.

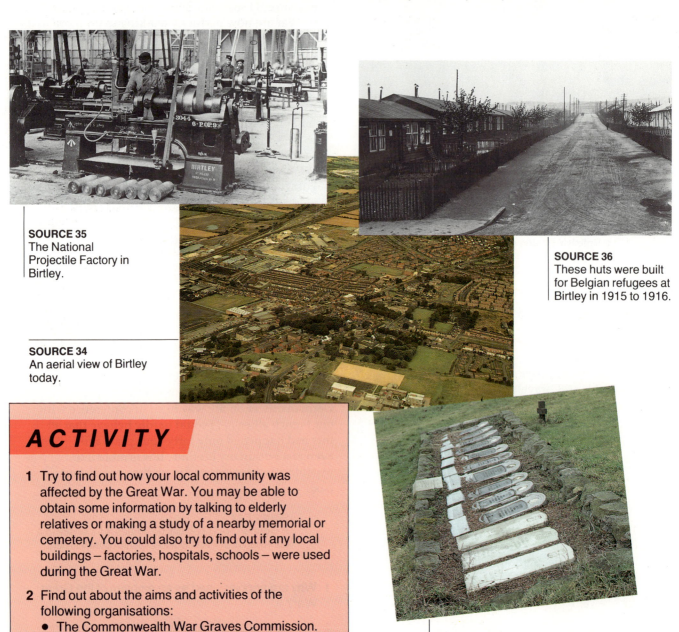

SOURCE 35
The National Projectile Factory in Birtley.

SOURCE 34
An aerial view of Birtley today.

SOURCE 36
These huts were built for Belgian refugees at Birtley in 1915 to 1916.

SOURCE 37
Graves of Belgian refugees in Birtley cemetery.

ACTIVITY

1. Try to find out how your local community was affected by the Great War. You may be able to obtain some information by talking to elderly relatives or making a study of a nearby memorial or cemetery. You could also try to find out if any local buildings – factories, hospitals, schools – were used during the Great War.

2. Find out about the aims and activities of the following organisations:
   - The Commonwealth War Graves Commission.
   - The Royal British Legion.
   - The Western Front Association.

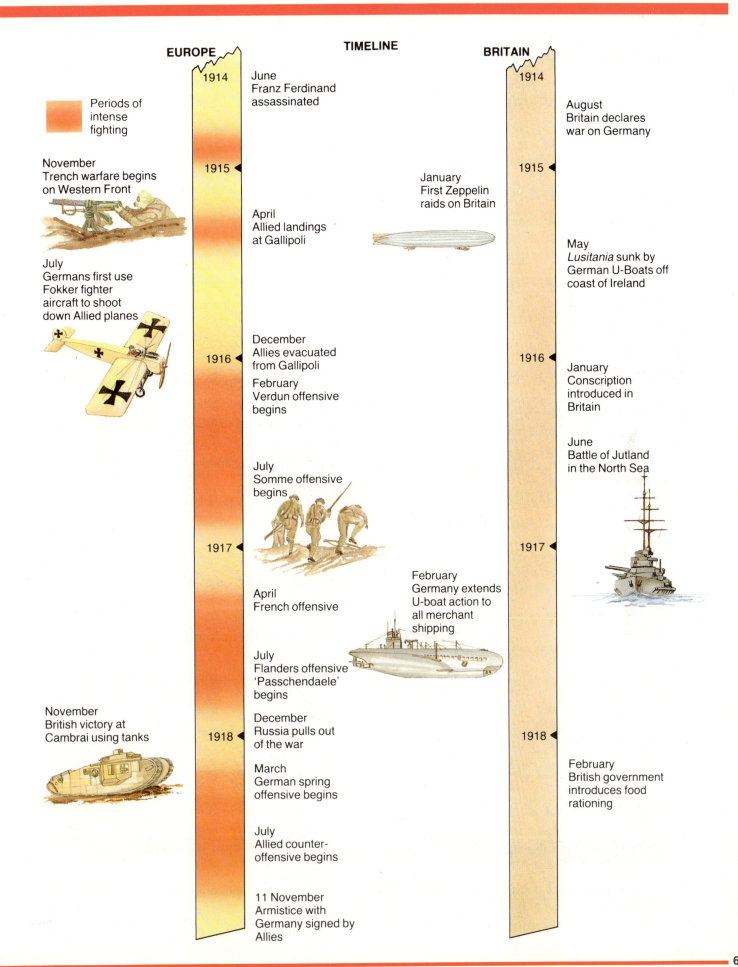

Glossary

Allies
Countries which support each other.

Ammunition
Missiles such as bombs, gas, bullets and shells.

Archaeology
Studying relics from the past, often items found in the ground.

Armistice
An agreement to stop fighting.

Artillery
Large guns used to fire shells.

Attrition
Wearing down the enemy by attacking over a long period, causing regular losses.

Cavalry
Troops on horseback.

Civilians
People who are not members of the armed forces.

Coalition
A temporary union between political parties.

Conscription
Compulsory military service during wartime.

Deployed
Sent into battle positions.

Duckboards
Wooden boards laid over the muddy trench floor.

Dugout
A shelter in the wall of a trench.

Fatigues
Domestic duties carried out by soldiers.

Fire step
The ledge in a trench which the sentry stands on.

Fraternisation
Being on friendly terms with the enemy.

Infantry
Troops on foot.

Kultur
German for culture, used sarcastically by the Allies.

Leave
A period of permitted absence from military duties.

Memoirs
An historical account based on personal experiences.

Mobilise
To prepare armed forces for war.

Munitions
All kinds of weapons and military equipment.

Neutral
A country which does not take sides during wartime.

No-man's-land
The zone between enemy trenches.

Offensives
Planned attacks on a large scale.

Ossuary
A monument built to contain human bones.

Patriotism
Being proud of your country.

Periscope
Instrument used to view above ground from a trench.

Platoon
A section of a regiment of about 30 men.

Propaganda
Information used to influence public opinion.

Rationing
Giving fixed allowances of food and clothing.

Reconnaissance
Surveying enemy positions to get information.

Relic
An object surviving from the past, an artefact.

Reparations
Payments made by the defeated countries after a war.

Sentry
A soldier who keeps watch for enemy attack.

Shell-shocked
A state of mental disturbance resulting from being exposed to the horrors of trench warfare.

Shelling
Bombarding with explosives.

Testimonies
Spoken or written reports of events.

Treaty
A formal agreement, binding to all who sign it.

Ultimatum
A final offer or warning issued during negotiations.

Unification
The creation of one country from a number of states.

Zero hour
The time set for the start of an attack.

Index

Page numbers in **bold** refer to sources/captions

aircraft 17, **25**, 33, **33**
alliances 7
ammunition 15, **15**
Amritsar Massacre 55
archaeology 23
armistice 51
Arras, Battle of **44**, **52**
artillery 12, 15, 17
Asquith, Herbert, 21
attrition 37, 45-46
Australia 21, **43**, **57**
Austro-Hungarian empire 7-8, **8**

Balkans 7, **8**
barbed wire 15-16, 38, **38**, **47**
battlefields 22-23, **22**, 36-48, **57-59**
battleships **6**, **7**, 24
Beaumont Hamel 22-23, **22-23**, 39, **39**, **59**
Belgium 9, 13, 31, **31**, 45, **45**
Birtley **60**
blackouts **25**
Bolsheviks 45
Bosnia **8**
Britain 6-7, 9, 21, 24-35, 53-55, 59-60
Brittain, Vera **56**

cavalry **12**, **14**-15
Cenotaph **42**
censorship 26-27, **27**, 43
chaplains 20, **20**
children **29-30**
civilians 24-35, 50, **54**
coalition government 21
conscientious objectors **34**
conscription 47
convoy system 49

Defence of the Realm Act (DORA) 27
desertion 44-45, **45**
disease **19**, 21, 54, **54**
Dix, Otto **17**, **57**
Dreadnought, HMS **6**
dugouts 18, **18**, 38

Eastern Front 14-15, **14**, 45, **45**, 50
enlistment 10-11

families 30, 42-43
Ferdinand, Archduke Franz 8-**9**
films **40**, **57**
Fitzgerald, F. Scott 22, **23**
Flanders **44-45**, **57**, **59**
Foch, Marshal 51

France 7, 13, **26**, 31, 38
fraternisation **20**
funerals 42-43

Gallipoli 21, **21**
generals 32, **32**, 52-53, **52-53**
Germany 6-9, **13-14**, **24**, 49-51, 56-57, **56**

Haig, Sir Douglas **32-33**, 45, **46**, **51-52**
heroism 32-33, **43**
High Seas Fleet 24
Hindenburg Line 44, **44**
Home front 24-35

India 55
Infantry **12**, 15, **38**, 51
influenza **4**, 54

Jutland, Battle of 24

Kaiser Wilhelm II 9, **27**, **46**, 51, 56, **56**
Kitchener, Lord 10-11, 16, **21**

Laffin, John **52**
leave 30, **30**, 32
Lloyd George, David 21
Lüdendorff, General 16
Lusitania 26, **49**

McCrae, John **59**
machine guns 12, 15-16, **15**, **39**, **51**
media 26-27
mines 16-17, **16**, 38
mobilisation 10-11, **10-11**
mourning 43
munitions 15, **15**, 21, **28**, **40**
mutiny 44

Nash, John **48**
Nash, Paul **17**, **19**
nationalism 7-8
naval blockades 49
Nevinson, C.R.W. **15**, **19**
Newfoundland Memorial Park 22, **22**
no-man's-land 17-18, **20**, 32, **38**
North Sea 24
nurseries 29, **29**

offensives 36-46, 53
Owen, Wilfred **48**

Passchendaele, Battle of 45
patriotism 10-11, 28
peace campaigns 34-35, **34-35**
Pétain, General Philippe 32, 36, 44
photography 27

poison gas 16-17, **16**, **27**, 39
poppies 59, **59**
propaganda 26, **26**

rationing **4**, 31, 49, 54
Red Baron 33, **33**
refugees 60, **60**
Remarque, E.M. **5**
Remembrance Day **42**, 59
reparations 56-57
Royal Navy 6, 24
Russia 7-8, 14, 45

Sarajevo 8-9, **9**
Sassoon, Siegfried **19**, 35, **35**, **43**, **52**
Schlieffen Plan 9, **9**, 13
schools **4-5**, 27
Serbia 8, **8**
shells 15, 17, 22, 23, **40**, **51**
shell-shock 35
shortages 30-31, 48-49, 54
Somme, Battle of the 16, 32, 38-41, **38-41**, 57
Somme, German occupation **4**, 31
Somme, war memorials 43, **58**
supplies 15, 18, 49

tanks 16, **16**
Taylor, A.J.P. 35
Terraine, John **53**
torpedoes 49
trench warfare 12-23, 26, 32, 38-41, 52-53

U-boats 49, **49**
unification 7
United States of America 26, 49, 51

Verdun, Battle of 23, 36-37, **36-37**
Versailles, Treaty of 56-57, **56**

war memorials 43, **58**
Wells, H.G. **12**
Western Front 13-14, **14**, 20-23, 34, 36-48, 50-53
Western Front Association 59
Wilson, Woodrow, US President 35, 56
women 28-30, **28-30**, 35, **35**, **54**, 55, **55**

Women's Peace Conference (1915) 34-35

Ypres, Battle of 13, 16, 43

Zeppelins 25, **25**, 33, **33**

© Collins Educational, an imprint of HarperCollins*Publishers*

Peter Fisher asserts the moral right to be identified as the author of this work.

All rights reserved. No part of this publication may be reproduced, stored in a retrieval system, or transmitted in any form or by any means, electronic, mechanical, photocopying or otherwise, without the prior permission of the publisher.

First published in 1993 by CollinsEducational
77-85 Fulham Palace Road
Hammersmith
London
W6 8JB

ISBN 0 00 327239-7

Cover design by Glynis Edwards
Book design by Liz Black
Series planning by Nicole Lagneau
Edited by Helen Mortimer
Picture research by Diana Morris
Production by Ken Ruskin
Artwork by John Booth (pages 4-5, 8, 15, 36, 42, 44, 58, 61 and poem borders), Peter Dennis/Linda Rogers Associates (pages 7, 9, 21, 24, 38 and 53), Angela Lumley (motif artwork on pages 6, 12, 24, 36 and 50)

Typeset by Dorchester Typesetting Group Ltd

Printed and bound by Stige-Arti Grafiche, Italy.

Acknowledgements

Every effort has been made to contact the holders of copyright material but if any have been inadvertently overlooked the publishers will be pleased to make the necessary arrangements at the first opportunity.

Photographs The publishers would like to thank the following for permission to reproduce photographs on these pages:

T = top, B = bottom, R = right, C = centre, L = left

After the Battle 22R; Airfotos Limited 60C; Barnaby's Picture Library 33T, 42B, 58TL; Bayerisches Armeemuseum 14T; BEAMISH: The North of England Open Air Museum 60TL & TR; Graham Bradbury 26C; British Film Institute 57B; Cambridge University Library 34/35; Commonwealth War Graves Commission 58TR; Culver Pictures 26B; Peter Fisher 10T, 22L, 23, 59, 60B; Fitzwilliam Museum, Cambridge 35R; Galerie Nierendorf, Berlin 17L; Hulton Picture Company 32C, 33BR, 45T, 54L&R, 55T; Illustrated London News 32T; Imperial War Museum, London 3, 4, 6R, 10BL&R, 11, 13, 14B, 15T, 16, 17R, 18, 19, 20, 21, 25, 26T, 27, 28, 29, 30, 31, 36, 38/39, 40, 41, 43, 45B, 46, 47, 48, 49, 50, 51, 55B, 56; Mary Evans Picture Library 7T, 33BL, 37L; Military Picture Library 6L, 22T; Musée de la Guerre, Paris 44B; Popperfoto 8T, 34C; Staatliche Museen zu Berlin, Preussischer Kulturbesitz-Nationalgalerie 57T; Tate Gallery, London 15B; ZEFA 37R.

Cover photograph: Imperial War Museum, London.

The author and publishers gratefully acknowledge the following publications from which written sources in this book are drawn:

After the Battle for an extract from Rose E.B. Coombs, *Before Endeavours Fade*; Cambridge University Press for an extract from Gill Thomas, *Life on All Fronts*, 1989; Leo Cooper for an extract from H. Sulzbach, *With the German Guns*, 1973; Faber and Faber Ltd for extracts from Siegfried Sassoon, *Memoirs of an Infantry Officer*, 1930; Robert Hale Limited for an extract from Nigel Jones, *The War Walk*, 1983; The Controller of Her Majesty's Stationery Office for an extract from Crown copyright material held in the Public Record Office (WO 95/2308, Newfoundland Regiment War Diary); The Imperial War Museum for captions from the film *The Battle of the Somme*, 1916 (captions 8, 41 and 37), preserved in the film archive of the Imperial War Museum, Lambeth Road, London, from whom copies of the film may be purchased on video-cassette or rented; Thomas Nelson for an extract from Stuart Sillars, *Women in World War I*, 1987; Oxford University Press for extracts from James Munson (ed), *Echoes of the Great War: The Diary of the Reverend Andrew Clark 1914-1919* © James Munson, 1985; Dr A. J. Peacock for extracts from 'A Rendezvous with Death', *Gun Fire* issue number 5, 1986; George Sassoon for poems by Siegfried Sassoon: 'The Hero' and 'The General'; Sidgwick and Jackson for extracts from Malcolm Brown, *The First World War*, 1991; Alan Sutton Publishing for an extract from John Laffin, *British Butchers and Bunglers of World War I*, 1988; Mr John Terraine for an extract from John Terraine, 'The Generals', *Stand To!*, 1982; Virago Press for an extract from Vera Brittain, *Testament of Youth*, © Paul Berry, The Literary Executor of Vera Brittain, 1970.